morality

To Rose Mendy
From Rev Dr Michael-C. Mkpadi
Chaplain, African & Caribbean Chaplaincy
Leeds Diocese.

BEING REAL

Teen Life and Christ
Teens and Spirituality
Teens and Relationships
Teens and Morality
Teens and Society
Teens and the Future

teens and morality

JERRY SHEPHERD

BEING REAL

Saint Mary's Press™

Genuine recycled paper with 10% post-consumer waste.
Printed with soy-based ink. 5091900

Nihil Obstat   Rev. Patrick J. Boyle, SJ, PhD
             Censor Deputatus
             November 1, 2004
Imprimatur: †Most Rev. Raymond E. Goedert, MA, STL, JCL
             Vicar General
             Archdiocese of Chicago
             November 2, 2004

The nihil obstat and imprimatur are official declarations that a book or pamphlet is free of doctrinal or moral error. No implication is contained therein that those who have granted the nihil obstat or imprimatur agree with the contents, opinions, or statements expressed, nor do they assume any legal responsibility associated with publication.

The publishing team included Lorraine Kilmartin, development editor; Mary M. Bambenek, development administrator; Mary Koehler, permissions editor; Lynn Riska, typesetter; Kimberly K. Sonnek, designer; Getty images, cover photo; manufacturing coordinated by the production services department of Saint Mary's Press.

Printed in the United States of America

Printing: 9 8 7 6 5 4 3 2 1

Year: 2013 12 11 10 09 08 07 06 05

ISBN 0-88489-840-7

Library of Congress Cataloging-in-Publication Data

Shepherd, Jerry, 1949–
  Teens and morality / Jerry Shepherd.
      p. cm. — (Being real)
ISBN 0-88489-840-7 (pbk. : alk. paper)
  1. Catholic youth—Religious life. 2. Christian ethics—Catholic authors.
I. Title. II. Series: Shepherd, Jerry, 1949– Being real.
BJ1249.S445 2005
241'.042'0835—dc22
                                                      2004018469

CONTENTS

PREFACE

This book is one in a series of six books about teenagers for teenagers by a non-teenager, so most teenagers will be immediately suspicious of it. After all, many adults talk to teenagers as though they were a foreign species, far beneath the adult's normal sphere of experience. And no one of any age enjoys being talked down to. You can handle a lot of that patronizing when you're a little kid, but the adult pose wears thin as you get older and realize that adults do some pretty stupid and childish things themselves. In fact, the adults who do the dumbest things are often the ones who enjoy lecturing you the most.

I do hope that I'll avoid such talking down in these pages. The fact is, having worked as an educator among teenagers for many years and still having some very clear, often painful memories of my own teen years many eons ago, I really don't feel that superior. I want to talk with you person to person, as an equal, as a friend, as one who has known, respected, and learned from many young people.

But, the teen radar counters, what are you selling? Adults are always trying to get teens to fulfill adult expectations, to conform to what adults propose, to be nice little boys and girls who don't ruffle any feathers. Adults seem to want teens to stay under their thumbs and dependent for as long as possible.

True as this motivation may be in some cases, I hope it's not true for me. Obviously, I have a vision of life that I'm anxious to share with you. My credentials are simply that I have experienced more than most teenagers have just by living longer and that I have had the good fortune to know many teenagers rather well over the years. Such experience doesn't necessarily make me any wiser, but I hope it has given me some perspective on life. It is simply this perspective I want to share with you in these pages. My aim is that you become more independent and free-spirited. You can buy some or none of what follows. I certainly can't force you. Even if I could, I wouldn't, because then the vision would be of no value to you. You have to decide yourself whether to buy into it.

This book is also suspect because it is about religion and the teenager, and, for many teenagers, it is simply not cool to show interest in organized religion. Though many teens are interested in spiritual matters, they often believe that religion is something that's not quite real. At least, it's not as real as everyday experiences like family, friends, foes, school, parties, love, hate, anger, desire, and frustration. But I have called the series Being Real because the main perspective I hope to persuade you to accept is that Catholicism provides the most real understanding and evaluation of our daily experience as teenagers or at any age.

To appreciate this claim, we need the willingness to take a longer view of things. Otherwise, immediate events flood our minds completely. What I mean is this: see if you can now recall the occurrence that seemed the biggest catastrophe in your life, not in the very recent past but within the last year or two. Perhaps you failed an important exam or a course and thus blew a reward your parents had promised you. Or you got grounded for a month for doing something stupid. Maybe you missed an important shot or messed up your solo, ended up with a boring date for the school formal, smashed up the car after spending all your savings on insurance for it, got rejected by a college, or didn't get the job. When such events occur, they seem tragedies whose effects will never be effaced, the most real of real happenings in our lives.

But with time, with perspective, minor tragedies fade from our memories and become potholes in the overall course of our lives. A former student of mine once was grounded for two months and kept from playing on the basketball team because he brought beer to a party. Naturally, as a sixteen-year-old, he thought it was the end of the world. In his case, the incident also proved to be the spark for a vast improvement in his studies. A year or so later, I reminded him of it. "Gee," he said, "I'd forgotten all about that." This kind of standing back from our immediate lives to gain an important sense of perspective and proportion is what I try to help you do throughout this book.

Some of you have experienced tragedy and suffering in your lives on a larger scale than the examples I've given, and the vision I share in this book can help you find meaning and companionship in those kinds of tough times. I try in this series to show how the Catholic faith puts teenage life into a perspective that is both realistic and idealistic, one that satisfies the best of our human and spiritual desires and meets our deepest needs. The key to this vision of life is a real person: Jesus Christ. Christian commitment is, finally, a commitment of the heart and mind to Christ, who alone deserves that degree of commitment. We only dare claim that the Church is the most real of realists because the Church is the continuing visible presence of Christ, the most real of people, the pattern and power for all "being real." And it is Christ, who, despite knowing us through and through, challenges teens today, as he once challenged his followers in Galilee, to become more real.

Allow me to add two practical points. First, many quotations in the text are from the New Testament. I feel that the most effective way of getting to know and love the person of Jesus Christ is through an intelligent reading of the reliable written records of those first Christians who either knew him or knew others who knew him.

If you do not own a copy of the New Testament, I'd encourage you to buy or borrow one so you can see for yourself what it contains. If you are unfamiliar with the way of referring to parts of the New Testament, allow me to explain it briefly. You'll see in your New Testament that each book is divided into chapters and verses so that each bit of text has its own number. This numbering system was invented so that people using different editions of the New Testament in the same or different languages could refer easily to the same text. Pages wouldn't work because the same quotation number would appear on different pages in different editions.

The first part of a reference to a particular place in the New Testament names the book because the Bible is really a collection of what were once separate books. The first number after the name refers to the chapter or chapters of the book, and the second number, which follows the colon, refers to the verse or verses. Thus "John 14:16" means that the quotation comes from the Gospel of John, chapter 14, verse 16. "Mark 2:1–12" means that you'll find an example of Christ's claiming the power to forgive sins in the Gospel of Mark, chapter 2, verses 1 through 12. Check out that one now to make sure I haven't made a mistake.

Second, I have generally not quoted other sources in order to avoid clutter and slowing the reader down. But any idea you find valuable or useful in this book is not original; it comes from my study and readings in the Catholic Tradition of the past 2,000 years. That said, whatever you find confusing or "unreal" probably arises from my own limitations of thought and expression.

WHY
BE GOOD?

Why be good? Why am I told to behave in certain ways when my feelings go against those ways, when all the others are doing what they want and enjoying themselves, when the very people correcting me— my parents, teachers, priests—don't always agree and often act against their own advice? I mean, some adults warn me constantly about drinking, but then they go and get wasted at their parties. Doesn't that just mean they don't really believe the warnings themselves?

Why be good? Seems like there's nothing in it for me. So-called good people are unhappy losers. They don't go anywhere, don't do anything. They don't drink or smoke or go on dates. They never have any fun. Besides, I've tried to be good sometimes, and I can't do it. Maybe other people, more religious types can, but I can't. The rules are just there to frustrate me.

If you find yourself thinking this way, I have the following advice: STOP KIDDING YOURSELF. STOP WHINING. START ACTING LIKE A REAL MAN OR WOMAN. I know this sounds harsh, but I'll admit I want to shake you up a bit. I will explain these objections to being good later. But if you don't set them aside at least temporarily from the outset, you'll miss the overriding issue at hand: How can I become a better person? Wouldn't you like to become a better person if possible? The moral law enables us to do so and applies to you, to me, and to everyone—whether we like it or not—just the same as gravity— except moral falls maim us much worse than physical falls. The moral law is not a hypocritical plot of adults to keep you under their thumbs. It is a pathway to true goodness and enduring happiness. Adults have to struggle as hard as you do to stay on it.

Oh, I know. Hundreds of voices—advertising, media, friends—are telling you morality—especially sexual morality but, really, every other type, too—is out of date. Your own experience seems to say the same. If you could get in trouble, tell a lie. If someone's not just like you and your group, mock him or her for a laugh. If someone is showing off a prized possession, steal it, destroy it.

But those voices—aren't they a little suspicious? Advertising has one purpose: to get you to buy. Peers who urge you to do wrong have one purpose: to use you, to provide companionship for their projects. Adults who tell you to do what feels good, to try out new "lifestyles," have one purpose: to try to ease their own consciences by getting others to imitate them. None of these people has your best interests in mind.

"But I know people who do supposedly immoral things, and they seem pretty happy," you may say.

The key word here is *seem*. Scratch the surface a bit, catch them without their public pose, and you'll see some real unhappiness. Tune in on their lives later or at the end, and see how happy self-indulgence in the things of this earth has made them.

Sometimes we deliberately forget about God and morals and goodness, and we commit a particular serious sin and—nothing happens. The sky doesn't fall, no bolts of lightning pierce us, nobody gets on our case, nothing but that irritating little voice that keeps accusing us—which we can, thank God (thank who?), ignore. So we may think, "See, it's not true that sin hurts me."

But breaking the moral law has consequences as real as those that occur when we break a physical law. If you run full speed into a brick wall to show your defiance of material structure, chances are you will crack some bones. If you deliberately detour off the roadway of the moral law, attracted, perhaps, by an apparent shortcut to self-fulfillment or some pleasant looking grove, you will definitely crack some spiritual bones. Some breaks are just more obvious than others—at first. You get drunk, you suffer a hangover. You give someone a hard time, and they give it right back to you. You steal some-thing, you're teaching others to steal from you. But even if you don't always recognize consequences right off, they exist as losses in your own self-respect and inner peace, in your interior relations with others—especially God. Cancer, too, spreads quietly and unfelt—until often it's too late.

"But some of the bad things I've done have been enjoyable."

Of course. God made the world good, nothing in it is bad. If things weren't good, they wouldn't attract us. It's our misuse of them that makes our action wrong. A teenage boy once asked me, "Why did God make women so beautiful?" He was struggling with purity. But we're supposed to admire beauty in people—they reflect God's beauty. We're supposed to be attracted to the other sex—otherwise, friendships, marriages, and babies would never be made. The prob-lem is when we allow ourselves to lust after others, seeing them as objects of our own pleasure, not as human beings with dignity and worth. What lasting effect have you gotten from your indulgences so far? Have they satisfied your desire for good things? Have they made you happy? Have they made you a more loving person? Isn't the heart of them selfish self-seeking? Have you harmed or used someone else for your pleasure?

Goodness

Think more about your experience. What is goodness? What does it mean to be good at a game, a sport, or anything? First, it means there is at least one right way and at least one wrong way to do the thing. There's a correct way to shoot a jump shot so it gets over the defender and through the hoop. And there's a way of falling forward and pushing the ball that guarantees failure. If there weren't right and wrong ways of playing a sport, how could we say that someone is a bad player and someone else is a good player? Goodness implies an accepted standard that anyone who is serious about a game, a job, or a skill will try to live up to.

Second, to be good at something must take an effort. Given our fallen human nature, if something can be done in a right way and an easier, sloppier, wrong way, our laziness will tend to opt for the second. But if we really want to play the violin, we'll need to practice and practice what seems awkward fingering and bow movements until they become second nature. Only then will we be good violinists.

If we can talk about moral goodness at all, it means that there must be a right way and a wrong way to live our life day to day. Otherwise, how can we say that one person is good and another bad? How can we distinguish morally between Hitler and Mother Teresa? How can we say that when Sarah spread that untrue rumor, she acted badly, but when Paula stuck up for us, she acted well? Morality is about behavior. So moral goodness means that there is a right way and a wrong way to behave. And we'd expect, once again, that this goodness would not come easily or completely naturally, and that we'd often have to make a conscious effort to practice it.

Of course, for a Christian, the answer to questions about goodness should be clear. As we've seen in other books in this series, Christ, the most real person, tells us how to be real people and that following the moral law is part of it. We also realized that Christ was not a "goody-goody" and that he doesn't want us to be, "goody-goodies". He wants us to be good because, in the long run, we will be more real and happy and will have more attractive personalities. We fulfill our true destinies, become most ourselves, by willfully channeling our fallen minds, drives, and desires in positive ways.

Our struggle to imitate Christ includes following his moral teaching and life. Morality is the first path to happiness—the spiritual life calls us beyond morality but builds on and grows along with it. In fact, we can live the moral life fully only when we have God's grace. The spiritual life and moral life become really one in practice—like dance partners who merge to perform beautiful patterns. When we try to live the fourth commandment better and be more respectful of our parents, we can also do it for love of God and offer God the self-denial involved. Such acts for us are not just good in themselves but draw us closer to Christ.

But we can think about moral life separately from the spiritual life. People always have been and always will be concerned about right and wrong behavior, even if they never hear of Christ. Philosophers, even godless ones, have argued for centuries about what makes a good person and a good life. First, people could be and were aware of right and wrong before God's revelation. Today, we can still discuss moral issues—at least, those in the daily papers—with people from other faiths or with no faith.

Considering morality separately in these pages can also help us focus more directly on the issues behind the critical teen attitudes expressed at the beginning of this section. I try to do so in three chapters. The first, "Laws and Legalisms," considers the nature and role of law, especially the natural law, which is summarized in the Ten Commandments. The second, "Moral Actors, Moral Acts," reminds us of the facts about the human psyche, the role of the mind, will, and feelings in moral life, and what makes an action good or bad. The third, "Paths of Glory," discusses the virtues, the specific trails we must follow to become real men and women, especially those that may be particularly difficult in the teen years, such as chastity, sobriety, and joy. A very brief fourth section urges us to moral heroism. As usual in this series, I rely on both experience and the person and teaching of Christ to guide our thinking.

LAWS
AND LEGALISMS

The Extremes of the Law

As teens, most of us have a curious love-hate relationship with the laws and rules that society, the school, and our families impose on us. On the one hand, laws often seem to exist just to constrain us, to make us uncomfortable, or to prevent us from having a good time. As we become more independent, we tend to test the limits of these laws, to see how far we can go without getting caught or punished. The most apathetic teenagers can develop an energetic cunning when they are bent on getting around a parental curfew, a school's dress code, or a town's speed traps.

On the other hand, we want clear, consistent dos and don'ts. We quickly cry "unfair" whenever adults make up rewards and punishments as they go along. In fact, most teenagers don't really resent reasonable rules so long as they bind everyone equally. We feel the need to be organized by outside authority if we are to achieve anything in groups, because few of us want to exercise authority over our peers. As students, we respect teachers whose rules are clear, fair, and consistent. As athletes, we respond best to coaches who establish explicit routines and expectations. As workers, we want to know what we are responsible for and when.

Both teenage attitudes—wanting the order of law but resenting some of its constraints—are normal and common in adults also. In theory, I think most everyone would agree that carrying either of these views of law to an extreme does not make much sense. But because, as teenagers, we tend to extremes, it's useful to consider them.

Legalism

On the one hand, excessive reliance on the law becomes legalism. Everything ought to be covered by rules and regulations, and we should always "go by the book," no matter what the circumstances are. From this mentality arise impossibly tangled bureaucracies and mindless, unnecessary rules. Worse, legalism produces petty, near-sighted authorities, who harp on the unimportant and miss the essential:

- teachers who weigh the format of a paper more heavily than content or style
- coaches who pay so much attention to details of organization that they forget to teach the basics of the sport
- clerks who make us wait forever as they check a form, only to tell us that we're at the wrong window
- parents who suddenly recall some very minor lapse in our behavior as a reason for not letting us go on a big date

Legalists distort reality by claiming something is true and just when it really isn't. It is true, for example, that we did misbehave in that one case. But it is not true or fair that such a small incident should be held so heavily against us that we miss the big dance. Legalism is often a tool for abuse of authority.

Of course, teenagers play that game too, when it's a question of self-interest. We argue that we should be allowed to go to a certain concert because four years ago our parents let our older brother go to a similar one, even though he was younger than we are now. We conveniently forget, and hope our parents will also forget, that our brother's concert was downtown while ours is four hours away. We insist that we should be able to drive our father's good car. When we got our license a year ago, he said he'd let us if we proved a good driver, and, after all, we haven't gotten into any real trouble . . . except for those two speeding tickets that don't count because the court didn't put them on our record. There's no harm really in trying out such arguments so long as we realize we're playing a game and don't become addicted to distortions of reality.

Anarchy

At the other extreme, normal resistance to the law becomes anarchy. Why can't everyone just do his or her own thing, we wonder in certain miffed moods? Why shouldn't we be allowed to stay out as late as we want if we get up and take care of our basic school and home duties—well, more or less? Why should the city have curfews for minors or put up all those stupid four-way stop signs? On a deeper level, why should the state have the right to force me to register for the draft or to pay income taxes? Why does the Church claim the power to tell me how I should behave on a date? Why can't I just do whatever I want with my money and body? I'm free, aren't I?

Even in such moods, we are dimly aware of the difficulties with anarchy. Let's say, for example, that Arthur walks into a grocery store where we work the cash register, waving a gun and threatening to drill us unless we hand over the cash from the till. Luckily, for us, he trips over some electrical wires, and our coworkers subdue him.

"Now, wait a minute," says Arthur. "I was just kidding around. No harm intended, and none given. As a matter of fact, you harmed me by having these electrical wires all come together near the entrance to the store like that. And I really could have been hurt when you all ganged up on me. That wasn't fair, and, in fact, I'm going to seek damages myself. Besides, no one is going to arrest me, and no court on earth has the power to punish me."

Let's assume Arthur is correct, and there are no laws, courts, or police. Who would decide what actions are "harmful," and how would they determine it? What if Arthur defines "harm" differently from us and restricts it to the physical? Then we harmed him, but he didn't harm us in any way. If we could agree to get twelve peers to judge between us and agree again as to which twelve, they might all have different definitions of harm. And how would they figure out how much weight, if any, to give various circumstances: that Arthur's children are starving, that he was temporarily crazy with grief over his wife's walking out on him, or that the gun wasn't loaded anyway? Finally, might they not just decide for Arthur because he's a friend, a relative, or a nice looking guy?

Because there are no laws and no courts to apply them to specific cases, no one can be judged guilty. But even if Arthur were found guilty, how exactly would we punish him? Who would determine a just penalty and its length? Who would have the right to impose it? to lessen it? Who would protect you and how, if he seeks revenge? We couldn't decide any of these matters without the law.

Anarchy distorts reality by pretending that all law is purely arbitrary, that there is nothing in the nature of man or society by which to distinguish justice from injustice. Some of the laws and rules we commonly break are indeed arbitrary and minor. Going ten miles over the speed limit on a clear highway is not, in itself, immoral, but other laws are necessary and reasonable guidelines for just and moral behavior. Stealing others' property or maliciously publishing untruths about someone are both illegal and immoral. To get in the habit of excusing ourselves from following such laws is to invite the kind of unfair chaos, where there is no right and wrong, that we have seen in Arthur's case.

Christ and the Law

Christ in the Gospels also rejects these two extreme views of the law. For him, true law is necessary and just because it is based on reality, but it should not become legalistic. For the Jews of Christ's time, the most important laws were those contained in the Old Testament and those the official commentators developed from it through the centuries. Christ obviously respects the Law, which is, in fact, the word of God, and everything rightly derived from it. He claims that "until heaven and earth pass away, not one letter, not one stroke of a letter, will pass from the law" (Matthew 5:18). He refers the rich young man to the commandments of the Old Law as the first steps towards holiness (see Matthew 19:17–19). And yet he obviously dislikes the kind of bureaucratic, petty, boring legalisms of those Pharisees who give more importance to the letter than to the spirit of the Law.

An incident near the beginning of Mark's Gospel clearly shows the Lord's disdain for mere legalism and its sources:

> Again he entered the synagogue, and a man was there who had a withered hand. They watched him to see whether he would cure him on the sabbath, so that they might accuse him. And he said to the man who had the withered hand, "Come forward." Then he said to them, "Is it lawful to do good or to do harm on the sabbath, to save life or to kill?" But they were silent. He looked around at them with anger; he was grieved at their hardness of heart and said to the man, "Stretch out your hand." He stretched it out, and his hand was restored. The Pharisees went out and immediately conspired with the Herodians against him, how to destroy him. (3:1–6)

The Jewish religious officials taught that no work should be done on the Sabbath, the Lord's Day. This is a reasonable, if not strictly necessary, deduction from the third commandment of the Decalogue, "Remember the sabbath day, and keep it holy" (Exodus 20:8). But the Pharisees, known for strictly observing the Law, defined work so narrowly that their teaching prohibited many acts of justice and charity on the Sabbath. In the passage above, their hypocrisy is multiple. First, these Pharisees actually want Christ to heal the poor man so they can accuse him of breaking the Law. Second, Christ's questions to them highlight that their restrictions are not the true law of Moses but their own overly literal applications. Third, they are supposed to be faithful to God's ways, but they have no concern for the man's plight. Fourth, they witness a miracle that could only have been worked by the power of God, but, rather than rejoice and give thanks for it, they run off to plot the destruction of the miracle-worker.

In other words, they really care nothing at all for the spirit or letter of the law, or for the sufferer. This type of legalism really riles teenagers. It prohibits something good only, it seems, because it is something good, or, at least, not in accord with some petty authority's mindset. But our Lord's anger and grief at such narrow-mindedness exceed ours, because the Lord knows, infinitely better than we do, what real goodness is and how responsible authorities should promote it.

Christ also clearly endorses the letter and the spirit of the true, permanent law. As the supreme lawmaker, he interprets and even adds to it. Saint Matthew shows us Christ insisting that he has not come to abolish but to fulfill the laws and the teachings of the prophets (see Matthew 5:17). Jesus's words release the hidden potential of those laws and show how new demands arise from them. For example: "It was also said, 'Whoever divorces his wife, let him give her a certificate of divorce.' But I say to you that anyone who divorces his wife, except on the ground of unchastity, causes her to commit adultery; and whoever marries a divorced woman commits adultery" (Matthew 5:31–32). "Good and gentle" Jesus is a pretty tough customer when it comes to clearly distinguishing right and wrong. Indeed, his exercise of this authority in his own right, rather than in the name of some other authority or text, distinguishes him from the Scribes and Pharisees and points to his divinity. Who would dare tighten up the law of God or separate it from man-made legalisms and merely temporary regulations, except a madman or God?

The Natural Law

As we saw earlier, without law we would have chaos, each man and woman simply doing what they felt like doing without any coherent means for settling even the simplest matters of justice. We need the government's civil law to protect our rights, to decide legal right and wrong, and to ensure that all members of society are treated fairly.

Even laws that are arbitrary and changeable usually have that aim. Most traffic laws, for example, concerning speed limits, stop signs, passing and no-passing zones, and the like, do more than simply ensure a certain minimum of orderliness. They seek to protect innocent life and limb from nuts driving madly all over the place, in whatever lanes and at whatever speeds they wish. All good laws promote some aspect of the common good. They contribute in some fashion to the physical, economic, social, cultural, and spiritual development of the individuals in that society. To be just, however, civil laws must reflect, or at least not contradict, what traditionally has been called the natural law.

The natural law includes principles that express a fundamental sense of morality that God has placed in human beings. The natural law declares that humans have rights and responsibilities related to their dignity as persons. It follows that some actions are just and others unjust. Because people are worthy of a fully human development, the natural law enshrines the rights to life, food, housing, work, raising a family, and so on, that are necessary for life and development. Because people are spiritual beings that have a dignity beyond the purely material, the natural law insists that you can't treat them like things.

The Church sees the natural law as God's law for correct and fruitful human behavior. It contains the Maker's instructions to the user: follow these if you want your self—your very self—to work right. All peoples, says the Church, can know the natural law by reason alone, without God's revelation, especially as it has been "written on their hearts" and consciences (Romans 2:15). Christian apologists, writers who defend and explain Christianity, like C. S. Lewis in *The Abolition of Man* and in *Mere Christianity,* have tried to show that the natural law endures in all cultures and times.

The Ten Commandments

The Ten Commandments state many of the main principles of the natural law. The first three reflect the fact that human beings were created by God and are completely dependent on God for their nature, existence, and preservation.

1. I am the Lord your God: you shall not have strange Gods before me.
2. You shall not take the name of the LORD your God in vain.
3. Remember to keep holy the LORD'S Day.

(Catechism of the Catholic Church, p. 496)

The Ten Commandments tell us that real people, those who are responding to God's plan for their lives, recognize God and what they owe him as creatures.

The remaining seven commandments are the basic principles that should guide human relations in society:

4. Honor your father and your mother.
5. You shall not kill.
6. You shall not commit adultery.
7. You shall not steal.
8. You shall not bear false witness against your neighbor.
9. You shall not covet your neighbor's wife.
10. You shall not covet your neighbor's goods.

(CCC, p. 497)

Real people, the Ten Commandments tell us, don't disobey legitimate authority, kill or harm the innocent, commit improper sexual acts, steal, tell lies, or even internally lust for their neighbors' spouses or possessions. Just as the first tablet shows what we owe God in justice, so the second tablet shows what we owe one another and ourselves in justice. Real people, they imply, live virtues like piety, honesty, chastity, respect, temperance, and all the rest.

We need the natural law to guide us to goodness and happiness, because we are fallen and imperfect creatures. You know how in climbing mountains you often have several choices of trails? Only one will take you to the top. Insist on a different one, despite what the guidebook says, and you end up like some friends of mine—stuck on a steep peak and in need of forest rangers to get them down. Refusing the path of the natural law may make for easier going for a while, but eventually leads to a humiliating isolation far from the summit of God's desires for us.

Again, the commandments of the natural law are like signs on the highway telling us which way to go to reach a certain city. We can ignore them and take the opposite road, but we won't reach our city. The signs are there as a help to us. They're not restricting our freedom but allowing us to freely reach our goal.

Obviously, the natural law does not mean following all our "natural" impulses. That would be fine if human nature were intact as God intended it to be. Then, if you felt angry, you could vent that anger because it must be just. If you felt hungry, you could eat without worrying about overdoing it. But the natural law recognizes that the effects of original and personal sin have split wounded human nature and tilted it towards defiance and sin. It recognizes that we are free to ignore the right course of desiring and acting. The natural law, like the civil, assumes that people, despite their dignity, are not naturally and instinctively good at all times—otherwise, you would not need laws to protect human rights and worth. You wouldn't need to be reminded of the natural law. You wouldn't need to correct or be corrected for blameworthy behavior.

The very form of laws suggests the potential both for good and evil in people. Laws remind us, as rational creatures, of things we must do to be worthy of our dignity, and command us, as limited beings, to avoid doing things that violate our dignity and that of others. "Honor your father and mother." Note that the subjects who are to give this honor are "all of you" and that the people worthy of this honor are "all who are fathers and mothers." "You"—all of you—"will not kill"—any other human being. We can't protest that we feel that the person we killed was worthless and had no right to live. The law, both natural and civil, says that the man we killed was a human being with God-given dignity, and therefore worthy of life. We acted immorally.

I'm sure at this point, some of you may have questions.

Someone might ask, "If this natural law is so clear, why do we need to discuss it at all?"

The only honest answer is because we so often act stupidly. We think of short-term pleasures, instant gratification, and ignore long-term consequences. We pig out now even though a moment's reflection would remind us of the stomach problems we had the last time we did so. Also, we can lie to ourselves about our own actions, strive to erase the memory of what's right and wrong. We've been all against lying until we feel forced to lie once. If we lie often enough, lying becomes a habit and seems second nature. So we make excuses for ourselves, rationalize our actions. Finally, there are offspring of the main principles that we might not understand without a reliable guide. Basketball is simple in the main—shoot more baskets than the other team—but can get quite complicated in the various ways you can score. You need a knowledgeable, articulate fan to explain these. For Catholics, that guide must be the official teaching of the Church.

"If this law is part of human nature and can be known by unaided reason, why does God bother to reveal it?"

God gives us the commandments so that all might have a complete and authoritative understanding of the demands of the natural law. Thus, we can better resist the blindness of the fallen human mind and the will to try and get around them or to twist them. The Ten Commandments highlight the "grave," or most serious, obligations we have toward God and toward others.

God's knowledge of God's law, that is, God's total understanding of the nature and operation of the universe, goes far beyond natural law. God has chosen to reveal another part of it, the law of love, which could not be reached by unaided reason. The heart of this revelation in the New Testament is that God, whom we might have understood by reason as an impersonal creator and sustainer, is actually Love. Indeed, God is three persons in a community of absolute love and the model for all our earthly community life, starting with the family. Our relation to God, then, is not that of zombies before an impersonal force (YES, MASTER!), but that of friends and lovers who keep God's commandments out of love and trust.

That last point needs some reflection. Catholics should behave morally because the revealed divine law and the natural law are, in fact, commandments of someone who, as our Maker and Redeemer, knows and loves us completely. When you were a little kid, you probably got mad because your parents wouldn't let you cross the street by yourself or go too near certain dogs or wander out on the soccer field when a game was in progress. Later, you understood that your parents actually were looking out for you. They showed you what was and was not good for you, because they loved you and knew your nature and the world's better than you did.

God's commandments, too, are really a loving Father's indications of what will prove good and what will be positively harmful for our full development and happiness on earth and in our much longer life with God thereafter. Saint Augustine even suggests that if we truly loved God, we would not need any law. We would simply do selflessly what we thought God would want us to do because that would always prove best. Unfortunately, few of us ever reach that degree of sanctity.

"But does everyone buy this idea of a common natural law?"

No. Many people today deny there is such a thing as a universal moral law of human nature. They have a variety of reasons for this attitude. Some simply don't believe in a Maker and so don't believe in God's laws. Others say we cannot know any objective law because we cannot know anything about nonphysical, nonmeasurable things like goodness, honesty, and friendliness. Still others claim laws are just a matter of mutual agreement or custom. They are current conventions and could be otherwise.

But that some actions are always wrong just seems common sense. Think about it! Suppose someone steals a coat out of our locker. We'd be pretty upset if we went to school officials to report the theft and they said: "So what? It's just your opinion that stealing is wrong. Some people think stealing is fine." Even those who don't buy the natural law in theory, appeal to it in practice—especially when they're the wronged party. You may claim to disbelieve in the universal application of the Ten Commandments, but when you're robbed or physically threatened or lied to in an important matter, you appeal to the corresponding commandment quickly enough.

Many of today's great social issues are debates over the natural law. The Church's views on abortion, euthanasia, homosexuality, marriage, biogenetic engineering, and the like, are not just matters of faith but also of a reasonable view of humanity's nature and purpose. We should have hope that we can convince others of the truth in these matters.

We discuss current social issues in more detail in *Teens and Society,* another book in this series. Here we want to focus on our individual selves as followers or nonfollowers of the natural law. We need to know how we make moral decisions and what makes them good or bad.

MORAL ACTOR, MORAL ACTS

Ever see little kids refusing to get in the car to visit relatives with their families? Maybe something "bad" happened to them the last time they visited—a cousin picked on them, a grandmother was too affectionate, or an uncle scolded them. Or maybe they have their own agenda —they'll stay at home and play all the video games they feel like, undisturbed by parents or by siblings fighting for their turn. Whatever the cause, such kids stubbornly refuse. The parents escalate from coaxing ("Grandma will have that cake you like") to ordering ("Young man (or lady), you will get in this car immediately!") to threatening ("If you don't get in this car *now*, you'll never watch TV for the rest of your life!"). Or clever parents might say, "Okay, fine, if that's what you want, you stay here all by yourself while the rest of us go." Now, if such kids were actually left by themselves, chances are they'd get bored with video games pretty quickly. The hours would seem like days in their isolation, and they'd probably be crying by the time the family returned.

We are like those little kids before God. God's laws show us the way to undeniable true goodness and happiness—not Grandma's cake, but joy beyond our knowledge. But because God made us intelligent and free, because we can allow ourselves to be led irrationally by our feelings, we can judge something else—our favorite video game—of more value and refuse God's gifts. We can even think, will, and feel our way into total isolation from the warmth of God's family.

With this sense of how important moral life is for being real—and thus for our happiness now and in the future—in this section we will discuss the role of these three human elements—our intelligence, free will, and passions—in moral decision making.

Thinking Life Through

We can know right from wrong. For example, we should easily understand natural law principles and their immediate consequences, as summarized in the Ten Commandments and our Lord's moral teachings—in theory. To use this knowledge in the real world, God has given us a conscience, the practical intelligence to recognize moral situations and to recall and apply appropriate moral principles and reasoning to them. Conscience first alerts us that a particular situation requires a moral decision and then enables us to make the proper judgment. A friend asks us to go with him to a music store to help him shoplift his favorite artist's latest CD. We should be morally awake enough to realize that this is an instance of stealing and that stealing is wrong. Judging 99 percent of the moral decisions we have to make in day-to-day life is this simple—if we know the commandments and the basics of Catholic morality derived from them. We'll usually realize—at least, after the fact—when we've acted uncharitably, intemperately, or dishonestly.

Of course, we may occasionally face more complex situations. (I'm speaking here of real moral questions—not the theoretical ones of the three-people-one-space-in-the-lifeboat variety.) We've promised a friend we won't repeat something he's told us, but now we're being pressed about it, and so far keeping quiet, but are afraid the friend might be hurt unless we reveal the secret, or that we'll be forced to lie, and so on. If such cases confuse us, we should seek advice about the moral principles and practice involved.

Questions already?

"I thought you're always supposed to follow your conscience. Like, if your conscience tells you something is Okay, then you can do it."

We are supposed to follow our conscience—if we have taken the trouble to form it according to the objective moral law. Don't forget—conscience is our practical intelligence. We have a natural knowledge of right and wrong, but we can twist that knowledge to fit our whims. Unfortunately, some people have had the idea that there are no absolute wrongs hammered into their heads so much that they either can't, or pretend they can't, recognize even obvious sins. We can all be tainted by this mentality.

And then, of course, there is rationalization. An unmarried teenage couple has it all figured out: "We have sex because we really love each other and really feel sex adds to our relationship and makes it take on a special beauty." Subjectively beautiful or not, it's wrong. If you don't know why, we'll discuss it in a later section. The point here is that we can't just make a claim of following our conscience to justify any action—adultery, theft, murder—because it seems or feels right in certain circumstances.

The Church claims to exercise the authority to teach what is right and wrong. She urges us to consult the experience and learning of a priest, older Catholic, or book that is faithful to the teaching of Christ and the Church. The reason for the condition is obvious: the Church can guarantee only those moral principles and experiences that she proclaims in the name and power of Christ. If anyone within the Church claims the right to preach conflicting "truths," then that person is not teaching with the authority of "the way, the truth, and the life" but only with the shaky authority of, let us say, poor Father Pride or Sister Vanity.

"Wouldn't it be better not to know what is a sin and what isn't? That way you could do stuff and not be in the wrong."

Sorry, we can't stay in the dark about moral matters. We all have the obligation of forming our consciences. We must study the teaching of the Church. We must seek advice from legitimate authorities about moral issues and temptations that confront us. We must be sincere in the sacrament of Penance and in our prayerful consideration of moral situations. We can't kid ourselves with the idea that what we don't know won't hurt us. Just not wanting to know hurts us.

And it will hurt us. Ever try to cut wood with a power mower? I don't think it would work very well! Oh, it might be fun to try, but all you'd end up with is a busted mower. Morality tells us how the human machine is meant to operate. Ignore the instructions and it gets busted—more and more. In Catholic morality, you cannot do anything you think might be sinful. You must find out before you act. If you are hunting and see a movement in the bush but are not sure whether it is a person or an animal, you're obviously obliged to find out before firing your gun. If you're a reporter and are told a bit of incriminating gossip about a public figure, you must find out if it's true before even considering printing it. It is the same with other moral issues. What kind of touching is allowed in a romantic relationship? Affectionate snuggling may be fine, but the kind of touching that arouses the sexual organs is only appropriate if the people are married. Is kissing okay? Well, it depends on what you mean by "kissing." If it's the type that necessarily arouses normal people, no. But kissing that's a sign of affection is fine. You must find out what the Church officially teaches from an authoritative source. And bear this in mind: you're not going to invent any moral situations, no matter how original or bizarre they may seem to you, that the Church has not encountered innumerable times before.

"Yah, but how can the Church understand my situation?"

Do you really think that no one has ever suffered what you've suffered, or felt like you've felt? In its two thousand years of experience, the Church has had to deal with many souls in many different situations. You'd be surprised how many Christians have struggled with the exact same issues you've had to face!

"But I mean, sometimes, even when I know the moral teaching and think I do love God, following the rules seems senseless and old-fashioned."

It's tempting to rebel against a teaching that you don't understand, or simply to ignore it. Yet in real life, if we trust someone in a certain field, we follow their lead, even if we don't quite get the point. If we have an English teacher who is a great writing instructor, we'd be silly not to heed his suggestions for revising a college application essay, even if we thought the essay perfect already. If we have a highly successful coach, we'd be idiots to question her strategy in the middle of a game, even if we didn't understand her strategy. Of course, for our own growth, we'd ask the teacher or coach to explain his or her reasoning at a convenient moment. But if we still didn't understand, we would go along with it because we trust that person's judgment and hope that we will understand in time.

In the same way, if we sincerely do not understand a point of Church teaching, we have the obligation to seek explanations. But if serious study still doesn't clearly resolve the issue for us intellectually, we finally have to trust the Church. Why? Again, because she speaks for Christ: "I will give you the keys of the kingdom of heaven, and whatever you bind on earth will be bound in heaven, and whatever you loose on earth will be loosed in heaven" (Matthew 16:19). And what does Christ ask of us? "If you love me, you will keep my commandments" (John 14:15). We must obey the commandments of Christ and his Church if we love him and want to be like him and with him.

"I came that they may have life, and have it abundantly" (John 10:10). The aim of Catholic moral teaching is to make us more fully human and more fully Christlike. We follow the commands of Jesus through his Church—and not the world's immoral, selfish demands and ever changing opinions—so that we might live as true men and women in touch with reality and come to the glory of a resurrection in Christ. Again, if we could think, judge, and love perfectly, we would not need such guidance. We need it because we are weak and so often try to wander off across the street or playing field by ourselves, risking life and limb.

Going to Sunday Mass

Let's look at a typical example of rebellion: teenagers who find Sunday Mass boring and don't want to go. "Why," they may ask, "can't we just love God on our own? or go to Mass on any day we choose? What difference does it make?" The Church's reasoning is quite clear. From the very beginnings of Christianity, it established Sunday as "the Lord's day" because that was the day of Christ's Resurrection. At the very least, says the Church, we can keep it holy, as the third commandment urges, by attending the sacrifice Christ established for showing our respect for God, union with God's Son, and solidarity with all Christians. Here, we will all be reminded, in a visible way before God, that we are part of God's people and of Christ's Mystical Body, individual grains that help make up the whole host.

Remember: Christ himself gave the Pope and the bishops the power to "bind" and "loose," to make necessary rules for the People of God, to determine what is and what is not in keeping with being a member of the Church. Attendance at Mass on this one special day each week is a kind of minimum requirement for a practicing Catholic—just as you need to pass, not excel in, a certain number of courses to be a graduate. (Of course, if you aim to just pass, you can easily fail.) Finally, at the deepest level, the Church supposes, and the individual Catholic should recognize, that obedient attendance at Sunday Mass is an act of faith, hope, and love in and for Jesus Christ. Realizing this, the teenager may learn to pray at least these acts during the Mass and soon find it less boring than he or she imagined. We don't go to church to be entertained. We go to tell God how much we love God and to be changed, through the Eucharist, along with our whole community, into more loving people ourselves. Now, even if all these explanations do not sink in completely at first, we still should fulfill the requirement because we trust in the Church, as guided by the Holy Spirit promised by Christ. "When the Spirit of truth comes, he will guide you into all the truth;" (John 16:13).

But perhaps we are only pretending not to see the point of a law such as Sunday Mass attendance because we simply don't want to follow it—just as we often pretend not to hear our mother's cry to be back at a certain time as we rush out the door, car keys in hand. How often do we claim intellectual difficulties with moral teachings, when, in fact, we just don't want to give up a habit of pride, laziness, or sensuality? Can't we see that we are really pitting our small, selfish will against the real love and trust that we have towards Christ? Isn't it true that we are practicing a kind of defiance against God by insisting that we don't need what the Sunday Eucharistic celebration has to offer us?

So one principle in the moral life is to trust the Church, and not the general culture, as the guide to our own understanding of that life. The Church either is or isn't Christ's embodiment on earth. You can't have it both ways, saying you accept some of the Church's moral precepts but not others.

A couple other principles are useful in making moral judgments. Some misdeeds can be like tripwires that set off a whole series of immoral explosions. They lead almost automatically to other misdeeds and so must be judged carefully. Excessive drinking or drug use leads easily to sins against charity, chastity, private property, justice, and even life. Why? Because our reasoning is badly impaired, our will weakened, our self-indulgence strengthened and eager for more. Are we more or less responsible for deeds that follow drunkenness or other highs? Definitely more responsible if we have gotten drunk or high knowingly and on purpose. In the same way, our often irrational dislike for someone can provoke us to sins of injustice, uncharity, envy, slander, and vengeance.

We must also be able to spot and avoid what are called occasions of sin—people, places or things that can, and perhaps have, lead us into trouble. If we know that every time we have gone out with a certain person, he or she gets us to misuse sex, then we must either convince that person not to misuse sex with us or simply not go out with that person. If we realize that every time we enter a certain store, we get an apparently irresistible urge to steal, then we must stay out of that store. The more we know ourselves—our tendencies, weaknesses, experiences—the more we can avoid temptations.

Free Will and Responsibility

The natural law, saintliness and sinfulness, reward and punishment all assume we have the free will to choose good or evil and are responsible for our choices. Without such an assumption, our whole civilization and its social, professional, and legal structures would topple. If no one were free, how could we possibly and justly hold anyone accountable for shoplifting, bribery, or even murder? How could I seek damages from the mechanic who was supposed to have fixed my car but didn't, and who therefore caused my accident? If he didn't have free will to do otherwise, then how is it his fault that my car wasn't fixed? No one would be really responsible for any of his or her actions. But we do hold others responsible for their actions: we do determine if they are guilty, and, if so, we punish them.

If we are mature, we accept our responsibility and the rewards or penalties that go with it. We got an A because we studied; we got a D because we didn't. We got a raise because we worked hard; we got fired because we didn't. We have good friends because we care for people; we have few real friends because we don't. But sometimes, like little kids, we try to justify our wrong actions by saying our passions, circumstances, genes, upbringing, whatever, just made us do things that were wrong. What we really mean is that we didn't have the willpower to say no to those influences.

All moral action requires not only an informed understanding of moral law but also a will that wants to love God who is the universal good above all things. The heart of sin, the saints and theologians tell us, is choosing self over God. All sin involves a freely willed turning away from God, in whom all creation can be enjoyed legitimately.

Instead, when we sin, we turn toward creatures, trying to make them serve as our gods. Of course, I believe in God—but what I really love are clothes, sports, parties, cars, beer, or my own ideas. We can sin. We can say no to God and selfishly isolate ourselves from God and others. If we say "no" definitively and never take it back, we get what we want: the solitary confinement of hell, alone with ourselves.

"Hey, wait! Isn't talk of sin and hell kinda out of date? Even priests seem to go out of their way not to talk about them."

Many people today don't like to speak about sin. Some may avoid the topic because they want to stress God's love, and sin and hell sound too negative. But they sound negative because they represent a very negative reality—the choice of self over God, a choice for which we should have a healthy fear.

Some think either that people cannot commit any real, conscious evil or that, if they do, it is not a breaking of a supreme lawgiver's commands. In other words, they don't believe in evil, in man's responsibility for it, or in God's existence or law.

But in our everyday experience, we know that we commit conscious evil as well as conscious good. We deliberately provoke our little brother or purposely plan to tell a lie. We have chosen to behave badly, to ignore a commandment, to lack love, to sin. We know we sin in many little ways each day and sometimes in serious ways. Even Christ's enemies had to admit that: "'Let anyone among you who is without sin be the first to throw a stone at her.' . . . When they heard it, they went away, one by one, beginning with the elders" (John 8:7–9).

Choices have consequences in real life. I choose not to do my work for a particular course, and I fail. I choose to do it as well as I can, and I pass or even excel. We know that our moral choices, our free decisions to do or not do God's will for us, also have consequences because Jesus promises several times that he will judge us. At the end of time, he will separate the sheep, who have loved others with deeds for his sake, from the goats, who have not. He will welcome the sheep into the bliss of his Kingdom. He will send away the goats, those "that are accursed . . . into the eternal fire" (Matthew 25: 31–46).

To judge us so, if we were not free to choose, would clearly be unjust. Christ thus confirms that sin exists and separates us from God and from others. We should hate sin as the greatest evil because by it we can kill the spiritual life, Christ's life and love within us, and choose hell.

"Why did God make us intelligent and free if we can screw up so badly?"

Because we can make rational, free choices, we can merit his praise as well as his blame. We can only prove our worth and love if we knowingly and freely choose good over evil, God and our true selves over evil, fallen selves. We don't compliment a computer on a job well done because it has been programmed to do it. It has no choice but to follow its program. We can't claim merit if we didn't do anything or were forced to do something. What if a teacher forced you to write a note of apology for insulting another student, but you really still think the other student deserved what you gave him? How much true repentance or reconciliation would be behind the note? If you're only moral because some one is forcing you to be, then are you really moral?

We do (or should) compliment students or workers on a job well done, because they have had to think it through and commit themselves freely to the project. They could just as easily have done it poorly. The God of Love wants us to follow the moral law freely and knowingly out of love for God—and a true love for those around us and ourselves.

To put it more simply: would you want someone to love you because he or she is forced to do it? Neither does God. God wants us to love God because we want to.

"But why does God allow us to be tempted to sin? Wouldn't our moral lives be a lot easier without temptation?"

Because of sin and our pride, we're prone to misuse our own good faculties and the good things of the world. We are tempted to desire things that aren't ours and to mistreat others who are children of God. God leaves us free to give in to those misuses but also the grace to refuse them. We grow when we freely overcome temptation.

Probably, like me, you have some acquaintances who are "know-it-alls," instant experts in everything from how to beat the next level in a video game to how to win a class election . . . until you challenge them to prove their knowledge by actually playing the game or getting themselves elected. We can say we love God, but until we actually have to make an effort to show that love, it is not really real—even to us. How do you know when someone loves you? Don't they show it by choosing to be with you rather than in doing other things that are tempting to them? Every temptation is a chance to show Jesus that we love and honor him over our misguided desire for false goods. We need tests to prove to ourselves how deep our love for God and goodness really is.

Having a temptation—a stray thought or desire, say, for wrongdoing—is not sinful in itself. Our imagination and memory will bring up, literally, the damnedest things at the most inappropriate times—but these are not sins unless we consciously consent to them. When we suddenly become aware that we're thinking of something sinful, we must resist it, or we will commit a sin. To resist it, we can use human means—occupying ourselves with work, energetically rejecting the temptation, imagining someone who would disapprove of it—and supernatural—a cry for help to Jesus, Mary, or some saint, a specific act of self-denial, recalling an appropriate spiritual quotation. If, with God's grace, we resist, then we've won a small victory over our fallen, twisted selves. If we give in, we should humbly recognize our fault and learn to rely on God's grace more. We ultimately win either way—we only lose when we refuse to recognize sin as sin and become stuck more in the mud. John Paul II has said that the loss of the sense of sin is a chief cause of society's moral and spiritual ills.

Temptations force us to face up to failings in our character and to do something about them when we might otherwise stay self-satisfied. The need to overcome obstacles prompts us to live closer to Christ and to develop his virtues. In human affairs, we've all admired people like Booker T. Washington or Helen Keller, who heroically overcame great sociological or physical challenges to achieve worldly success. The obstacles they faced even became a spur to their efforts. So should our recognition of our spiritual weaknesses in the battle for sanctity.

Christ and Freedom

What can Christ, the perfect man, teach us about this freedom to love truly? We saw in another book in this series, *Teen Life and Christ*, that Christ shows an incredible respect for freedom of choice and consistently refuses to force anyone, including teenagers, to follow him. He leaves the rich young man, whom he loves, the Apostles, who are as puzzled as the crowds by some of his sayings, and even Judas himself free to accept or reject his call.

But Christ's sense of his own freedom of choice is also incredible. He will lay down his life for others, but only when he is ready to. "No one takes it from me, but I lay it down of my own accord. I have power to lay it down, and I have power to take it up again" (John 10:18). His perfect self-determination is clear in those several strange episodes when he is threatened with something not in his game plan. His fellow townspeople, outraged that he identifies himself with the Messiah, wish to throw him over a cliff. "But he passed through the midst of them and went on his way" (Luke 4:30). Later, he does the same when a crowd wants to make him king (see John 6:14–15) and when the Pharisees wish to kill him for making himself equal to God (John 8:59). Again, the Jewish rulers send soldiers out to seize him. They return almost converted: "Never has anyone spoken like this!"" (John 7:46). Even when the time comes for his capture, trial, and condemnation, he seems to be the stage manager. Instead of forcibly preventing Judas from going to lead his enemies to him, Christ tells him to do quickly what Judas has already determined in his heart to do (see John 13:27). Instead of hiding from the soldiers in the garden, his powerful presence forces them to step back and fall to the ground (see John 18:6). Instead of being buffaloed by Pilate's brutality and power, he confuses and frightens the procurator, telling him he would have "no power over me unless it had been given you from above" (John 19:11).

On such occasions, Christ shows the perfect freedom of his divinity. Because he is goodness itself, he chooses the good necessarily. But he still can determine which of several goods to pursue and in what ways. If his plan for our redemption involves a certain time for preparing the Apostles and for fulfilling specific Old Testament prophecies, neither circumstances nor chance occurrences nor the plots of men will change it. Indeed, in all of the Gospels, there are only a few occasions when Christ seems to change his plan, as he does when he turns the water into wine at Cana and when he agrees to heal a Canaanite woman. In both cases, it is for the only reason that will ever move him: love. In the first case, it is love for his mother and her special intercession; in the second case, it is love for the woman's great faith. Similarly, theologians tell us, the Godhead creates freely and chooses what and how to create. God could have made centaurs if he wished or a whole world of creatures beyond sci-fi's wildest imaginings. Instead, he chose to create us and the world we live in.

But we do not necessarily choose the good. We act when we shouldn't and don't act when we should. We understand perfectly what Saint Paul means about the force of the "old self" within that so often prevents him from doing the good he intended. If we are sincere, we know with Saint Peter that we too can give in to "bombastic nonsense" and exercise a false freedom that actually makes us "slaves of corruption." We can pass off lust as love, drunkenness as being "the life of the party," meanness as honesty, and laziness in our work as being cool. "For people are slaves to whatever masters them" (2 Peter 2:19).

We know that we can make gods of our bellies, our envy, our pride, our comfort, or almost any passion for a short time or more or less permanently. In fact, Saint Paul sees Christ as becoming a slave in the Incarnation, because humanity was hopelessly enslaved to sin, to the various passions by which we can be ruled. We were not free because we did not have the power to choose the good consistently, and "everyone who commits sin is a slave to sin" (John 8:34).

One effect of the Incarnation, through the new and perfect God-Man, Christ, is our liberation from this slavery to the twisted self. Saint Paul even describes commitment to Christ as slavery to righteousness, which takes the place of the cheap enslavements to which our fallen nature tends (see Romans 6:16–18). That liberation begins with new, clear knowledge about ourselves and our new relationship to God. "I am the light of the world. Whoever follows me will never walk in darkness but will have the light of life" (John 8:12). "If you continue in my word, you are truly my disciples; and you will know the truth, and the truth will make you free" (John 8:31–32).

The heart of that truth is that God is our Father and is Love. We are to respond to God as Father and love as he has loved us. In our older brother Christ, with him, and through him, we will be empowered to achieve this liberation so we can live up to our potential as daughters, sons, and lovers. Without him, we remain slaves. The scars of original sin and the loss of rational and calm mastery over our various drives and powers will still hurt and sometimes overwhelm us. But his grace is sufficient for us to rebound (see 2 Corinthians 12:7–9), and, with continued efforts, to run the good race and capture the crown appointed for us before the world began (see 2 Timothy 4:6–8).

Freedom's Purpose: Serving God and Others

To understand freedom's purpose more deeply, think about our Lord's agony in the Garden of Gethsemane. Christ did not feel like dying for us. Foreseeing all the physical, emotional, and psychological sufferings that his torture and death will bring, Christ prays to his father that the bitter cup may pass. His human feelings, temperament, instincts all recoil from what is to come. Imagine it yourself: the savage whipping of your naked back, thorns pounded into your head, large nails hammered into your extended hands and feet. Imagine yourself, stripped of your clothes, crucified, bruised and bleeding all over, mocked by your enemies, betrayed by your friends, aware of the millions of desertions by us believers over the centuries. Christ knows that all this and more is to come.

And yet he does not want to escape unless it is what the Father wants: "Not my will, but yours be done" (Luke 22:42). He freely embraces God's will to serve in his Father's plan, despite everything pushing him away from it. His human mind sees the crucifixion is good and right, because it is part of God's plan, and his human will prevails over his human fears. He willfully rejects his instinct to self-preservation.

We too experience that our wills, enabled by grace, can triumph in the struggle to do good. Should we be surprised that living a moral and spiritual life requires an effort of the will? Isn't willpower necessary to achieve anything that is challenging or worth doing in life? If we wish to learn to play a sport or a musical instrument, to get an A in a challenging subject or a promotion in a job, we need the willpower to continue at it despite all the tugs of laziness, negative feelings, and mood. It would be great to be a pro soccer player, for instance, but, even for the gifted, the goal translates into hours of boring drills, learning how to play our position well, learning to kick and shoot with our weak foot, learning to head a ball properly, and learning to make accurate passes on the run. To achieve our freely desired goal, we must freely stifle the imagination that keeps presenting the difficulty of the task and freely "enslave" the negative internal forces to our will. Instead, as sports psychologists tell us, using our imagination to visualize ourselves doing something well can help us succeed: if we want to learn to ski, we should not just block out images of disastrous falls, but we should picture ourselves gliding effortlessly down the slopes. The point is, we need willpower to do anything good—we must will ourselves to stick with it and will ourselves to think positively.

Of course, anyone who plays a sport or has mastered a musical instrument knows joy as well. Although we do have to discipline ourselves to learn the skills we need, and to keep at it when we're tired, experiences of joy helps us stick with it. The runner feels great when she beats her personal best; the pianist delights in mastering a challenging score, the basketball player exults in the cheers from the bleachers and in his team's ability to build a strong defense.

"But that's my problem. When I want something, I really want it, I go after it 100 percent, whether it's studies, relationships, or sports. But that kind of leaves God out of the picture."

Not necessarily. There's nothing wrong with going 100 percent after a good thing as long as it doesn't prevent us from doing other good things that are duties of our situation in life. To go all out for an A in calculus is great, so long as we don't neglect our family and friends. God wants strong wills. In fact, Christ teaches us that the ultimate purpose and fulfillment of our freedom is to commit ourselves freely, 100 percent to doing the highest good, God's will for us, at each particular moment. If you'll give your strong will to God and God's service, God will use it to do many, many good things that, with God's grace, you can throw yourself into 100 percent.

Christ freely chooses to suffer and die for our sakes, to serve us in all our drastic needs: "No one has greater love than this, to lay down one's life for one's friends." (John 15:13). He shows us that the power of the liberated will is for us to do God's will and serve God and others freely. Like Christ, we are called to use our willpower to give ourselves to God and others—not just because we love others but also because we love ourselves in the right way. To find ourselves, to achieve our potential, to be real, to self-realize, or whatever you want to call it, we must give ourselves. Or to put it another way—God is love and generous self-giving. So to become like God we must give ourselves to God and others. God won't make us give ourselves to others. We must want to and actually do it consistently. We must become like Christ, who was a man for others.

"Well, how am I supposed to know what God wants from me? Is an angel going to suddenly appear?"

God's will for us is not totally mysterious and unfathomable, as it may seem in moments of confusion and loss. Normally, God's will is defined by where we find ourselves. Our mission now is to be the best student, the best son or daughter, the best friend, the best worker we can be in the specific academic, family, social, and job circumstances in which God has placed us—to be the best we can for love of God.

"So I don't have to wait around for someone to crucify me or something like that before I can give myself?"

No. Thankfully, we serve God whenever we serve God's image in others in the small ways life regularly presents to us. "And the king will answer them, 'Truly I tell you, just as you did it to one of the least of these who are members of my family, you did it to me'" (Matthew 25:40). Loving God and others, we will see dozens and dozens of opportunities each day to help out. Christ himself gives us examples of serving in little things. He criticizes Simon for not treating him courteously as a guest (see Luke 7:44–48), praises the servant who is trustworthy in a small financial matter (see Luke 19:17), and washes the feet of the Apostles at the Last Supper. "For I have set you an example, that you also should do as I have done to you" (John 13:15). We can serve God and others in school—helping a classmate understand a lesson or pick up dropped books, lending a pen or notebook paper, speaking kindly to someone who irritates us. We can serve God and others at meals—passing food as needed, listening to others, contributing appropriate conversation ourselves, telling a good joke. We can serve God and others around home—lending a hand with someone else's chores, playing with younger siblings, offering help on a project without having to be asked. Just imagine your normal day slowly and you'll see many such opportunities. And like the athletes and the pianist we pictured earlier, our "service muscles" will become stronger, and more and more we'll experience the joy that comes with serving and loving others. If we show our love for God by habitually keeping the moral law and serving others in our real, daily circumstances, we can, with God's grace, help build a true civilization of love.

Passions

Judging a moral situation and exercising our free will are not the only factors in our moral decisions. Our tricky passions can be a tremendous help or hindrance in the moral life. Passions are good in themselves, for they too come from our Maker. They are meant to reinforce our commitment to obtain true goods and to avoid true evils. The *Catechism of the Catholic Church* tells us that love is aroused when we see something good and desire it; similarly, we experience hatred when we see encounter evil.

> Love causes a desire for the absent good and the hope of obtaining it; this movement finds completion in the pleasure and joy of the good possessed. The apprehension of evil causes hatred, aversion, and fear of the impending evil; this movement ends in sadness at some present evil, or in the anger that resists it. (*CCC*, no. 1765)

Let's see how this summary applies to particular goods and evils in our lives. Think of something material, a new computer, for example. We'd love to have a laptop, which truly is a good and useful machine, and so we desire it and hope one day to get it. If we receive it for our birthday, we are pleased with the gift and start to enjoy the possession of it. Think of a physical evil, a bad flu, for example. We hate being sick with it from past experience and thus try to avoid it by frequently washing our hands and getting enough sleep—yet we still fear we'll catch it. Despite our precautions, we start feeling ill, get angry and try to will it away, yet finally are laid low and feel sad in our sickness.

Now think of spiritual examples. We love honesty, and we desire and hope to be honest. When we are honest, despite temptations to the contrary, we are pleased with ourselves and rejoice. We simultaneously hate dishonesty as an evil for those we deal with and for us. We turn away from temptations to it and have a healthy fear of our own weakness before it. We get angry with ourselves when we entertain temptations to it and sad if we give in to them.

"Okay, so these categories seem to work all right. Is there some problem with them?"

Ideally, our emotional life should always parallel our moral life. We should feel love, desire, hope, pleasure and joy in what is truly good, and hatred, aversion, fear, anger, and sadness towards what is truly bad. But we are fallen, and sometimes passions can hurt moral life.

First, they can blind our mind's judgment of what is right to do. Deep down, we know it's wrong to steal—but that digital camera is so cool, so much what we desire but can't afford, that we take it. We really do know we should show basic respect to everyone, but we hate those other persons so much for the way they talk or look at us, that we're constantly insulting them. Or we do something wrong and have the chance to admit it—but if we do, we'll be grounded, and we desire so much to go to see that new movie this weekend that we just have to lie.

We have to recognize this fact about ourselves: every temptation to go against the moral law will involve a desire for something that appears to be a good—and, if rightly possessed and enjoyed, is a good. Certainly there is nothing wrong with wanting a digital camera, or noticing failings (or what appear to us as failings) in other people, or looking forward to a decent movie. They become a cause for sin because we want to get or use them in a wrong way.

Passions can also blind judgment by making us forget that some goods are or can be more important than others. No material good is worth risking our spiritual welfare. (Just remember Christ's words about the worthlessness of winning the world but losing one's soul.) There are many wonderful material goods in the world—they all come from our good God, after all!—but none are worth embracing the evil of theft, murder, hatred, or lying. Nor can a Christian really justify, for example, putting self or career before God and family. What should come first in our loves and duties should come first in our concerns and actions. And please note: whenever we must choose between two real but apparently conflicting goods, we must judge the situation with our conscience, and not simply follow the one for which our feelings are strongest at the moment. We should not blow off a promise to help a friend move just because we've got an "irresistible" urge to go sunbathing.

Second, passions can control our choices if we let them. We tend to mistake our passions for will, feelings for commitments. Our society is a "feel good" one. If something feels good or seems right to us, then it must be okay. If we're sincere about it, we must be right. So, if I feel strongly about an issue, it doesn't matter if I harass or otherwise mistreat people who disagree.

Sometimes we're aware of the conflict between conscience and passions but still choose to let the passions rule. We know something is wrong . . . but we feel as though this occasion must be an exception. Violence except in self-defense is wrong—but this guy talks so egocentrically that we'd like to deck him. We must either will ourselves to follow our conscience and back off or to follow our dislike for braggarts and take a swing at him—immorally.

"But aren't our passions often instinctive? Like, if someone slams a door into my face by accident, I'm angry before I have time even to think."

Right, and because that initial reaction is instinctive, it's not right or wrong. It's only when we've had a second to think that we make a moral decision to contain our anger . . . or we make an immoral one by feeding our anger, willing it to grow. So—stop and think the next time you find yourself fuming over your little brother or sister's habit of messing with your stuff. Stop—and maybe say a prayer for the little snoop.

Third, passions can master us even in pursuing a true good or avoiding a true evil. Think of your athletic experience. When we're losing a match and the coach yells "Get mad out there!" he doesn't want us to go out of control. He wants us to use our passion, our desire for victory (a good) and anger at someone trying to keep us from it (an evil), to give us more drive. But if we do lose control, then passion takes charge and hurts rather than helps our play. We commit stupid fouls and may even have to be taken out of the game. In daily life, people may have healthy passions for many things—art, fishing, reading, trains, mysteries, you name it. All of these things are good in themselves. But we can lose control of our passions and become obsessed, completely absorbed by what really are limited goods. Then we focus so exclusively on this one good thing—which may even be a friend or a care-giving situation—that we neglect our duties and other good things.

In Summary . . .

The Church remains a clear voice against all such self-delusions. She tells us that the "morality of human acts depends on the object chosen, the end in view or intention, and the circumstances" (*CCC*, no. 1750). In other words, whether a specific choice is right or wrong depends on what we will do, why we will do it, and the situation surrounding our choice. So our feelings or sincerity may be taken into account under intentions. But, she further cautions: "A good intention (for example, that of helping one's neighbor) does not make behavior that is intrinsically disordered, such as lying or calumny, good or just. The end does not justify the means" (no. 1753). In other words,

whether an action is right or wrong in itself remains the first consideration in our moral decisions. If we know it is wrong and choose to do it
anyway, we can't excuse ourselves by appealing to our intentions,
feelings, or circumstances. We can't argue, as even some theologians
do, that a bad act is okay if its good results outweigh the bad. Or that
only a pattern of committing bad acts that indicates a total turning
from God is seriously sinful, while individual bad acts are not. The
popes and official documents of the Church continue steadfastly to
preach that "there are some concrete acts—such as fornication—that
it is always wrong to choose, because choosing them entails a disorder
of the will, that is, a moral evil" (no. 1755).

> It is therefore an error to judge the morality of human acts by
> considering only the intention that inspires them or the circum-
> stances (environment, social pressure, duress or emergency, etc.)
> which supply their context. There are acts which, in and of
> themselves, independently of circumstances and intentions, are
> always gravely illicit by reason of their object; such as blasphemy
> and perjury, murder and adultery. One may not do evil so that
> good may result from it. (No. 1756).

"But aren't there, in fact, exceptions to all moral laws? For example, if someone were literally freezing to death, couldn't he or she
legitimately steal clothing? Even murder has exceptions. We kill others
in a war and, in some places, we execute murderers, don't we?"

Those cases are not really exceptions to something sinful. They
are excluded by the very definition of the sin. To steal means to take
something that another person has a right to own, without their
permission. But no one has the right to deny to another the very
means of survival. To murder means to intentionally kill an innocent
person, that is, one who has not tried to kill you or in other ways
seriously endangered the community's safety. So there are no exceptions to actions that are always sinful. But there may be exceptions to

our basic human rights to things like property and life when the true good of others requires it.

"Okay, but say I commit a sin but don't realize that it's serious. Or I commit a sin without really thinking about it? I'm still guilty?"

No. Once we admit that the action is seriously sinful in itself, two other factors enter into judging our personal guilt. "Mortal sin requires *full knowledge* and *complete consent*" (*CCC*, no. 1859). It presupposes knowledge that the action opposes God's law and that the person has deliberately chosen to break God's law.

For example, some young people are taught that the only consideration for sexual ethics is whether the sex is safe or not. They may conclude that sexual contact other than intercourse is acceptable for them—and even good, because they believe such contact to be safe. Aside from the fact that any healthcare worker can tell you that intercourse is not the only way to pass along HIV/AIDS, genital sexual activity outside of marriage is a serious misuse of our sharing in God's creative power. But if the young person doesn't know that, the action remains sinful, but the person is not guilty of it. Still, as we've seen, we have to form our consciences by finding out which actions are good and which are sinful. In fact, "feigned ignorance and hardness of heart do not diminish, but rather increase, the voluntary character of a sin"[1] (*CCC*, no. 1859). If you're not sure, ask the priest straightforwardly in the sacrament of Penance, explaining simply, without going into unnecessary detail, what you've done or considered doing.

Let's now turn ourselves to the conditions for doing the good. Love, we have seen, requires us to give ourselves to the service of God and others. But to give ourselves, we must possess ourselves. To possess ourselves, we must detach ourselves from our many wayward desires. In a society used to instant gratification, we must learn to say no to our bad impulses, a control we can gain only by saying no sometimes to impulses that aren't bad. We need to struggle daily to grow with Christ's help in the various virtues so that we can ultimately experience the joy of doing Christ's will.

PATHS OF GLORY:
VIRTUES

For this very reason, you must make every effort to support your faith with goodness, and goodness with knowledge, and knowledge with self-control, and self-control with endurance, and endurance with godliness, and godliness with mutual affection, and mutual affection with love. For if these things are yours and are increasing among you, they keep you from being ineffective and unfruitful in the knowledge of our Lord Jesus Christ. For anyone who lacks these things is nearsighted and blind, and is forgetful of the cleansing of past sins. Therefore, brothers and sisters, be all the more eager to confirm your call and election, for if you do this, you will never stumble. (2 Peter 1:5–10)

To Be Like Christ

When you were little, did you ever dream of being just like your favorite basketball player? (Substitute your own childhood hero, if you prefer: your favorite pop star or Olympic gold-medalist.) Using the basketball example, you'd need extraordinary gifts: size, great health, strong hands, powerful legs. You'd need to get your mind, will, and passions all working in sync so that you could see your goal clearly and stick to it. You'd need the self-discipline of relentless practice of the basics—shooting, rebounding, passing, and defense—until the motions become second nature. You'd need determination, competitiveness, perseverance, willingness to endure pain . . . and many other virtues.

We can't all become the next hero of countless children nationwide. But there are as many potential saints as there are people.

Another book in this series, *Teen Life and Christ*, discusses how Christ calls all of us to become saints by imitating him, by becoming him. The process parallels the way we strive for any ideal.

Just as many great athletes have unusual God-given traits, so God gives all of us the extraordinary power of living Christ's life in the grace he won for us on the cross. But we must make the effort and use the means—prayer, sacrifice, the sacraments, and so on—to render those graces fruitful. You can read more about grace in *Teens and Spirituality*, also in this series. Our first step in response to those graces is to behave morally, which involves, as we've just seen, knowing right from wrong, wanting to choose the right consistently, and keeping our feelings working for and not against our moral judgments. (You can't "live in your head" to reach your potential in sports or morality.)

But being able to and wanting to reach our ideal in sports or moral living is not enough. We must get to know our strengths and weaknesses. We must go through the hard work of developing the right habits, which are called virtues, in the moral life. In both sports and life, we need the consistency of habitual excellence to be winners. It's of no use hitting nine of ten foul shots one lucky day but missing nine of ten for the following three days. To become a reliable foul shooter, it's not enough to know how to shoot properly and wanting to. We also must have the willpower to keep practicing and to control our feelings so that anger at failures, for example, fuels, rather than frustrates, our determination.

Likewise, if we realize we give up too easily in studies, we need to understand the virtue of fortitude and then really work at being tough on ourselves in specific situations, such as keeping at homework when TV tempts us away. We need to keep feeding our desire to win the battles, instead of letting our distaste for the effort involved undermine us.

In sports, we learn from experts, watching others, and perhaps reading about what works and what doesn't. In the moral life, the Ten Commandments, the classical notions of the virtuous life, and Christ and the Church's long teaching on both form guidelines for what is right and what is wrong. The virtues, good moral habits, are paths by which we attain a glory infinitely more desirable and important than mere human fame in sports or any other area.

Does living a moral life seem boring or dull to you, aimed at thwarting your natural impulses? Maybe. But be consistent. You'd have to say the same for the physical and mental efforts good athletes, gamers, musicians or successful people in any field must put themselves through to reach excellence. For an athlete or any other professional, the payoff is powerful performance. If a Christian keeps struggling to grow in virtue, the payoff is a truly balanced, happy, attractive personality in this life, heavenly glory beyond dreaming—and more. For the virtues lived in imitation of Christ are paths of fulfilling love as well as of glory.

So let Christ be your model in all the virtues. Read about his life. Talk to him in prayer. Seek his forgiveness and encouragement in the sacrament of Penance. Receive his very life in the Eucharist. Whenever in doubt about what to do, ask yourself, "What would Christ have me do?"

Improving Our Selves

Is there any one of us who wouldn't like to be a better person? There may be a few crazy people who think they are perfect, but normal teens know they can be better. They may resent adults telling them they need to improve, but, deep down, they know they have faults they ought to correct.

How could we be better? by getting more organized? by being kinder to certain people? by offering to help our friends more? by putting more time into studies? by trying harder in sports? by improving our appearance? by changing our behavior with a girlfriend or boyfriend? by taking better care of things? Take a minute now to make up your own list.

Our lists are really virtues that we need to grow in. You can call them good qualities or positive values, and that's fine, as long as we're all talking about the same reality. Virtues are those internal and external habits that make a person good. In fact, the word *virtue* comes from *vir,* which is Latin for "man" or "humanity." A person of virtue is a real human being because he or she exhibits the habits that are proper to humanity. To put it another way, what we admire in people are their virtues. We find them thoughtful, fair, honest, under control.

How do we become more virtuous? We must recognize several important points. First, moral virtues are simply good habits that have become so deeply rooted that they are second nature to us. (Vices, of course, are bad habits that have become similarly entrenched.) We develop them, as we develop any habit: by repeating them constantly. If we want to improve our backhand in tennis, we do so by taking backhand shots over and over again—in the right way. (Otherwise, we're just slipping further and further into the rut of a bad habit.) If we want to become more generous, we do so not by wishing it but by doing generous things whenever possible. One or two backhands made, one or two self-denying actions taken, don't make a habit. Consistency and a growing ease of execution do. We want to become generous, hard working, kind, cheerful, and the like, always, on demand, rather than occasionally, as though by accident.

Note also that although good habits cost us, they are always worth the pain of gaining them. For instance, the first day you ski is usually pretty miserable. You fall repeatedly, get covered with snow, laughed at, or, even worse, offered help by little kids, and totally frustrated by those stupid, awkward, impossible lengths of wood. You can't master the towline or chair lift; both must be stopped, and everyone sees you sprawling, unable to get up. It may be the worst day of your life. You'll never get the knack—the physical habits—of skiing. But would you really give up the exhilaration of swooshing down the big slopes, which you gain if you persevere? Virtues make us glad also. They give a spiritual pleasure deeper and more lasting than physical ones. Just recall how you felt the last time that, unasked, you helped—really helped—someone in difficulty.

Second, all of our desires to be better people assume there is a goal, a target to shoot for. The classical scheme of dozens of virtues, built around prudence, justice, fortitude, and temperance, helps us talk about the many ways in which a person should be good. It gives a map of the moral terrain, a guide to reach our goal of being better. It defines and allows us to focus on specific habits, thus breaking up the distant ideal into smaller, more doable steps. Just wanting to be "better" people doesn't help us much because "better" could mean dozens of things. But wanting to be kinder at home to our brother is specific; pinpointing behaviors we will do, such as using his name instead of that hated nickname, is even more clear, and certainly possible.

Now, it's true not everyone totally agrees on the ideals. Some, for example, may think that the virtue of fortitude or toughness means you bully everyone around to get your way—versus the traditional idea that, if you're truly tough, you never need to push anyone around, except yourself. Others might say that the only self-control you need with regard to sex is to make sure it's always "safe." The older classical meaning of temperance is that your drives, including sex, are never safe if you misuse them.

But, to the ordinary person, most of the virtues are still just common sense. Normal people don't think that acting unfairly or dishonestly, taking advantage of people, thinking only of yourself, and creating messes you don't pick up are good qualities. The virtues, as traditionally defined, are the embodiment of the moral life in people. Their practice makes us more truly human. If the moral law says you shall not kill, we normally live that command through the virtues of gentleness, kindness, patience, and charity.

Third, the model of the good person for Christians is Christ himself. Christ teaches us what people really are and should be. If we really want to be good, lovable persons, we must learn how to do so from Christ and his Church. Otherwise, given our great tendency to justify and make excuses for our bad habits, we'll easily end up becoming bad people. Worse, despite our vices and bad decisions, the world may see us and urge us to see ourselves as good people. Have you ever read or seen the movie *The Picture of Dorian Gray*, by Oscar Wilde? In it, a man who regularly indulges himself in a host of vices, still remains youthful, handsome, and vital. But a portrait made of him in his youth slowly becomes horribly ugly and distorted. Finally, the man cannot stand this foul image of what his soul has become and savagely rips it with a knife. He drops dead and turns into the portrait. We don't want to live a phony life even if the world applauds it. We want to lead a real moral life. To do so, we must understand and live the virtues.

Good Judgment

We have discussed many virtues elsewhere in this series. Here I'd like to focus on aspects of the four cardinal virtues—prudence, justice, fortitude, and temperance—that we may not develop elsewhere and on some virtues, such as forethought, purity, and sobriety, that can be especially hard for teens. The cardinal virtues are called cardinal not because they are the most important ones but because they are the hinges (Latin: *cardo, cardinis,* hinge) on which all the others ride. Without these hinges, the door to moral life barely opens, if at all.

Prudence reminds us that, for human beings, it is not enough simply to understand and to be well disposed towards the moral law. We need to make a habit of choosing the good. We need the capacity to judge the specific situations of our life by the light of the general principles of the moral law and to persist in the effort to live by those judgments. We may know, for example, that it's okay to kid our friends but wrong to speak to them uncharitably. But we need the presence of mind to distinguish one situation from the other, and the strength of will to shut up when we realize we should.

"How is prudence different from conscience then?"

Prudence is a habit by which we make all decisions, moral or not, taking the whole reality of the situation into account. For example, prudent people make considered decisions about what times are best for doing homework, in what order to do the subjects, who to ask to their birthday party, and so on. Conscience refers to our mind's judgments about practical moral decisions and, as such, is linked to the habit of prudence. Prudence, however, makes us not only listen to conscience regularly but also consider other aspects of the situation and actually carry the total decision out. For example, your conscience may tell you that you were in the wrong in a serious argument with a friend and that you should apologize. Prudence leads us not only to accept this judgment but also to decide how best to make up with the friend—is it more effective with this particular person to call or to wait until we can talk face to face?—and then to make the apology in fact.

A current dictionary will probably identify prudence with caution, timidity, and self-serving calculation. For example, a prudent investor is one who plays it safe and never takes risks on the stock market. But in traditional moral philosophy, prudent people may, in fact, do something quite risky if the situation demands it.

For example, take the case of a student at the beginning of the school year considering what clubs or activities to join. Some students are totally imprudent in arranging their time. Although they may have a full schedule of classes and an outside job already, plus a sweetheart with whom they simply must spend a lot of time, they rush about madly signing up for swimming, chess, newspaper, yearbook, and whatever else crosses their minds. Obviously, such people are not in touch with reality. We only have so much time and energy each week, and most of us can't bilocate. Therefore, we need to decide which activities are really the most important to us and forget the rest.

But prudent students might also decide to take a risk and over-extend themselves a bit for a good reason. For example, a young man might join the drama club precisely because he is afraid to perform in front of an audience. Joining the club will help him grow in self-confidence, even though he risks nervousness, ridicule, and, perhaps, failure. Or a young woman might sign up with a social services club because she knows she tends to get wrapped up in her own things that take a lot of time. The club will help her think more of others, especially those less fortunate than herself. In both cases, prudence tells the person to take a risk for the sake of the deeper good that will come out of it.

Prudent Christians are the most complete realists because they consider all the relevant aspects of a situation in making a practical decision. Such people judge with their minds and not just their feelings. They weigh the spiritual and moral aspects of a situation, as well as the purely physical and instinctive. The truly prudent will sometimes do things that seem utterly insane to those who are prudent only according to the world's standards. Recall Paul's decision to return to Jerusalem, even though imprisonment awaits him (see Acts 21:11–14). It seems crazy from a purely human point of view. Why not stay free and continue to do all the good he can? But for Paul, the most real part of the situation is what the Holy Spirit supernaturally is prompting him to do. Only much later do we get a glimpse of the Spirit's purpose when Paul writes that "what has happened to me has actually helped to spread the gospel" (Philippians 1:12). His imprisonment in Rome has led many others to preach the word and to make Christ better known throughout the city.

Truly prudent Christians will always try to take supernaturally objective views of their moral decisions. Should I cheat on this test or not? Should I go to this party that will probably be fun but will probably also get out of hand? Should I really listen to this music that is pretty blatant sexual or that promotes abusive attitudes? Should I repay Clare the money I owe her or just wait to see if she forgets about it?

Should I go to this place with my girlfriend, or will I just be asking for trouble? Should I goof off this hour that I'm supposed to be working for pay? We can multiply this list almost infinitely. We all make hundreds of similar decisions a week in small or big matters, and they are all opportunities to advance morally and spiritually or to lose ground.

Against Prudence

What real-life influences can weaken Christian prudence? Ignorance, for one. To make good, practical decisions, we need a knowledge of the basic moral principles, just as I must know something of the theory of automotive mechanics to fix this piece of junk that I call my car. Christian prudence assumes we want to know what Christ and his Church teach and are willing to study it, absorb it, and apply it. If we are really just going to do what we feel like or what the current fashions of the world tell us "everyone" should be doing, then we are hypocritical to pretend we want to live as Christ would want us to live.

Our experience of the secular world can also weaken prudence. The values the media present to us can be so skewed that we can come to accept sinful behavior as normal and natural. We can lose our appreciation for the wisdom of the Church and eventually lose all sense that there is anything to be prudent about. We may even come to consider those who are prudent as deluded, and "behind the times." For example, the current culture generally reduces sex to pleasure and so justifies almost any sexual activity . But the clear teaching of Christ and his Church is based on the obvious, biological fact that a primary purpose of sex is procreation within the commitment of a marriage, to bring new life into the world and to care for and educate it. Yet many who call themselves Christians have bought the "world's" view, hook, line, and sinker, and may even scorn and pressure others who try to be faithful to the moral law.

Sheer mindlessness is another enemy of prudence. Thinking requires effort. It's easier simply to follow instincts. Of course, if we're so virtuous that prudence has become like an instinct for us, then perhaps we can trust gut feelings. For most of us, though, instincts simply follow the path of least resistance to self-centered pleasure. We see someone with a super-sized Coke on a hot day, and we want one too. We rush to buy it without thinking at all, perhaps, if we have the time and money, if we'll be neglecting other duties, if we're being uncharitable to leave those friends who are with us, or if we might skip it and offer it up as penance. Obviously, there is nothing wrong in buying a Coke, but reflective people go against their instincts for good reasons. With regard to more serious moral decisions, the prudent person must stop and think, or similarly impulsive instincts will take over. Any of us might be tempted to to lash out in anger at someone who has hurt our feelings. The habit of prudence makes us stop for a moment, judge the act morally, and decide to ignore our instinct.

On the other hand, prudence doesn't necessarily mean a long, complicated thought process. Often a split second of moral consideration will show us the road to follow. I pass a particular store and think to go in to browse. But memory reminds me that every time I've done that in the past, I look at pornographic magazines and have troubles living purity. So I better avoid browsing or wait until I have something definite to get. In fact, a long thought process in cases like this often just means we're haggling between what we know we should do and what we feel like doing, between an objective long-term good and a subjective, immediate, short-lived satisfaction for our senses or ego or mood.

Pride opposes prudence if it prevents us from seeking and following the good advice of others. Yet common sense leads us to get other people's opinions in making decisions that don't involve moral issues. Before spending money to see a movie, most of us consult professional reviewers in the newspaper or on TV, and those of our friends who may have seen it. And we don't just consult any review or buddy. We get the opinion of those whose standards and judgments we trust and who have proved reliable in the past. If a friend tells us we have just got to see this hysterical new comedy, and we sit there bored out of our minds, then it's unlikely we'll trust that friend's advice on comedies again.

We should be humble enough to go through a similar process when we face moral decisions that are difficult, complicated, or new to us. Obviously, we wouldn't find it helpful to consult someone whose moral standards are as suspicious as that friend's judgment of comedy proved. Nor, if we are sincere, will we simply look for advisors whom we know will endorse our sin because they like committing it themselves. Rather, we will seek out someone who knows and lives morality, and has the disinterested authority to pass it on. Ultimately, as we saw earlier, that authority is the Church.

Fortitude

We need prudence to reach honest, informed, truly Christian decisions about what we should do or not do. But for us weak humans, making a practical decision is not the same as putting it into practice. How many times have we firmly resolved to follow a training program or diet or to break a bad habit, only to fall flat on our faces the next day or week? Fortitude is that virtue of the will by which we get up and try again and stick to the resolve until we've accomplished it . . . or at least done the very best we can in trying to. Fortitude calls for us not to be wimps in pursuing the good goals we set for ourselves.

Prudence is not a virtue usually associated with youth, because it benefits from experience that comes with years. But teens can understand aspects of fortitude better than most people because of their involvement in sports and games. Anyone who has participated in a competitive sport knows how long a season can be and how difficult it is to keep both enthusiasm and performance high. Inevitably, there are days when we simply don't feel like going through the same old drills and routines, when we'd just as soon stay in bed or get home early, when the weather is miserable and the prospect of success is bleak. Forcibly denying that part of our mind, will, or body that wants to call it quits, going against the grain, not once or twice, but habitually and whenever necessary, is part of the virtue of fortitude. Saint Paul himself, who, I suspect, was not much of a jock, uses the image of the persevering athlete as a model for Christian living: "Do you not know that in a race the runners all compete, but only one receives the prize? Run in such a way that you may win it" (1 Corinthians 9:24).

But Saint Paul also pinpoints the limits of the comparison. For athletes finally pursue only a "perishable" prize, where Christians pursue an imperishable one (see 1 Corinthians 9:25). We practice and practice until we attain the best conditioning and performance possible. We struggle to keep up our level of effort and teamwork for a long, hard season. Finally, we know the momentary joy and exaltation of winning, say, a division championship. What lasting benefit do we get out of it? clippings from the local paper? a trophy that soon is gathering dust in a corner of the living room? maybe a good-looking date for the prom? fond remembrances at class reunions? But even the world of sports asks: "Yeah, I more or less know what you did way back then. But what have you done for me lately?" And this gradual letdown exists only for the few fortunate winners. The great majority of athletes are necessarily losers.

No, suggests Saint Paul, great as athletic competition is, it can't begin to compare with the reward of moral and spiritual combat: life everlasting, where our joy will be full, and no one will take that joy away from us at any moment for ever and ever. In this race, no one needs to lose. Everyone can win, and everyone is given the means to win. And if we become less and less capable of competing in sports the older we get, we can always be youthful, always pick ourselves up to begin and begin again, in the "sport" of sanctity.

How strange, then, that often we will kill ourselves to win a mere earthly prize, but won't lift a finger to follow God's law that brings us to our true fulfillment and an imperishable prize! We will jog unfailingly day in and day out, get out of bed before dawn to be on the practice field or the rink, master our most difficult academic subject to maintain the required GPA, and generally work ourselves to death during the season. But we only laugh at the notion of self-denial for the love of God, neighbor, and our better selves! It seems as though our love for sport and work is greater than our love for the God who made these goods—made them, perhaps, so that we could compare them with the interior life and learn. We put our effort and commitment where our hearts are. To have greater respect for God's law, we need to give our hearts more to him. And the more we live and understand the law, the more we will see it as fulfilling all our heart's desires, until we, like the Psalmist, may exclaim, "Oh, how I love your law!" (Psalm 119:97).

Justice

Justice basically means that we give to others what we owe them—whether it is money, attention, respect, or deeds of service. I discuss justice in two other books in this series: in *Teens and Relationships*, I explore dealing justly with others on a personal level. In *Teens and Society*, I consider just social structures. Here I'd like to focus on piety and obedience, two virtues that are related to justice and that can be particularly challenging for teens to live.

We all have unequal relationships in which we definitely owe someone else something but cannot possibly repay it. For example, it might be an older friend who generously taught us all he knew about chess. Beyond showing gratitude, how can we make it up to them in kind? Piety is the virtue by which we give all we can to try to repay others who have given us the most important gifts. To whom do we owe piety? Our parents—no matter how much we do for them now or in the future, we can't repay their gift of life and nurture. Our country—because we can't repay the laws and institutions that protect our rights and make our continued survival possible. (Patriotism is a virtue—nationalism, "My country is always right, everyone else is wrong," is a vice,). And, of course, God—we can't repay God for our natural or supernatural life. We can't repay God for God's creative, redemptive, or sanctifying actions for us. On the other hand, before all these situations, we can't just throw up our hands and say, "Well, if it's impossible, I won't even try." Rather, piety teaches us that we must be willing to do everything possible to repay that debt, that nothing we do for those people can be excessive. (Provided it's moral, of course—we can't steal a diamond ring to give to our mother or rob a bank to save a church.)

Christian piety does not mean always praying in a church pew with folded hands. Doing God's will is the first act and responsibility of justice and piety. We can't treat people wonderfully and ignore God because we owe the Father, Son, and Holy Spirit infinitely more than any other persons. We are not in the real world if we don't recognize this primacy. Admitting it, we must act upon it by seeking to know and live God's will for us.

Piety means having this appropriate respect, a reverence for the persons of the Trinity. It's a form of justice, because it's really about giving God what is due God. We all admire certain people for their goodness. But God deserves our respect infinitely more than the worthiest person we know. So, in our direct dealings with God in the liturgy, we should be seriously attentive and responsive. When we attend Mass, we should follow and perform our role in the liturgy actively and consciously. We should prepare for receiving our Lord in the Eucharist through prayer and sacrifice, perhaps by reminding ourselves who God is and who we are, and we should thank God for God's benefits afterwards.

Of course, piety is central to the spiritual life. It leads us to regular practices, such as attending daily Mass and reading the Bible, which help preserve and express our loving attitudes toward God. It urges us to seize opportunities in our daily life for turning to God and offering our efforts to God. It helps us evaluate events in our life from God's perspective and to entrust them to God's care, even as, with God's grace, we try our best to respond to them well.

Why might all these aspects of piety be particularly hard to live during the teen years? Because teens tend to have the most nervous energy of any age group and "activism," that is, throwing ourselves unthinkingly into one activity after another, is a common enemy of piety. We must force ourselves to stop and think about what we are doing and why. We must remind ourselves of what life is about and its supernatural end. Here, such practices as daily mental prayer and making an examination of conscience can help us.

Christian Obedience

"Honor your father and mother." The fourth commandment implies attitudes and actions, including the virtue of obedience, that piety towards our parents requires. Now, we resist obeying anyone—not just as teens but throughout life. We have our rights, our dignity, our own opinions, and experiences. During the teen years, our rebelliousness tends to increase because of the greater awakening of our passions, minds, and desires for independence. But as always, we want to follow Christ's example.

Christ himself chose to live in obedience to his Father's will as a man. "He humbled himself and became obedient to the point of death—even death on a cross," says Saint Paul (Philippians 2:8). As a human being and the new Adam, Christ once summarized his whole desire on earth as wanting to conform to that superior will: "My food is to do the will of him who sent me and to complete his work" (John 4:34).

But Christ did not just obey his "Father's will." Amazingly, he also obeyed the will of his human mother and father, Mary and Joseph. He returns to Nazareth with them after they have found him in the Temple, and, Luke says, he "was obedient to them" (Luke 2:51). Thus, God, the Creator, obeys mere creatures all during God's teen years, for Christ is twelve at the time of his adventure in the Temple.

The New Testament and the entire Tradition of the Church tell us that, as teens, we must respect and obey all legitimate authority—parents, teachers, bosses, policemen—as coming ultimately from God. Like adults, we are obliged to obey it in anything that is not contrary to moral law. Of course, those in authority also have a serious obligation to exercise it responsibly and not to abuse it. (This teaching also applies to teenagers when they are left in charge of the house, an activity, or a job.)

Please notice that Christ's obedience is never the half-hearted form of legalism that we sometimes fall into when we're asked to do a chore, follow a rule, or anything else we don't feel like doing. We argue, we gripe, we make excuses, and, only when we're finally overpowered or outmaneuvered, do we give in. Then we drag ourselves resentfully, go through the motions, and fulfill, more or less, the letter of the law but not the spirit. There is little credit, little of Christ's generous spirit in this act. We are like some secure, overpaid athletes or film stars with long-term contracts, who just pretend to be trying. Not putting out, not committed to doing what it takes to succeed, not caring about or trying to spark the rest of the team or cast, they are a burden on the franchise or film studio rather than an inspiration. Christ shows us a full obedience that, when united to his cross and lived for love of him and of neighbor, can merit an abundance of grace.

Some teens might counter that they would obey their parents, as the teenage Christ did, if their parents were Mary and Joseph—but they're not even close. Because our parents are human, they can make mistakes in asking us to do things. They might be too rigid or too lax or a confusing combination of the two depending on the issue. But our instinct, despite our growing sense of independence, should follow our obligation to obey full-heartedly. Obviously, as rational creatures, we can try to discuss a matter calmly with our parents—shouting matches will never get either side anywhere and will upset the whole household to no purpose, as anyone who's in touch with reality will realize. (Must we not also admit that we sometimes get a perverse pleasure from causing uproars? We're getting back at our parents—for what? Trying to do their job?) Nor are we forbidden to use "psychology": picking the right time, circumstances, and parent to ask, sweetening them up with our behavior beforehand, and using intermediaries. Experienced parents will see through our ploys, of course, but may still be moved to grant our request. When they don't, when all legitimate maneuvers fail, then a Christian teenager can only accept the decision as part of his or her current state in life.

Of course, our obligation to follow our parents' indications doesn't last forever—in fact, only until we leave their homes. Good parents will give us increasing opportunity to make our own decisions and let us live with the consequences. They must do so when we are of age. But piety requires that we always respect them and hear out their opinions, often more informed by experience than ours.

Is disobedience to legitimate authority a sin? Yes, and in more serious matters, a serious sin. In fact, disobedience is the great grandparent of all sin and always involves the same pride that was at the root of Adam and Eve's fall (see Genesis 2:16–17;3:11). We are sure we know better, we who usually don't have the perspective and responsibility of the one in charge. We resist the control others seek to exercise over us, forgetting that God has "authorized" authority among humanity. Without it, the world would be entirely in chaos. Men and women would have no where to turn for learning, pursuing, doing, or preserving the good. Teenagers (and adults) must learn to trample down their pride and obey willingly and heartily. Remember: we never really lose in obeying, because we take another step toward holiness by embracing the cross of self-denial and thus becoming more like Christ, who was "obedient to them," despite his true divinity.

What if our parents or some other authority order us to do what is wrong? We can't be like the people who went along with Hitler's evil plans, can we?

No, of course you should never obey an immoral order. Fortunately this case doesn't come up in most teenagers' lives. If you think it does in yours, do make sure that the order truly is immoral and not just something that goes against your desires or feelings. ("Grounding," for example, is not immoral.) If you believe your parent is expecting you to do something immoral, then you will need to find the courage to seek help from a responsible adult, like your pastor or school counselor.

Temperance: Unreal Restraints?

For many teenagers, the Church's teachings on temperance, the virtue by which we moderate our natural drives for food, drink, sex, experience, and the like, seem the hardest to buy and to live. Here, if anywhere, the teen questions the realism of the Church and wonders how she can be so out of touch. How, after all, can a normal, modern couple enjoy themselves without some passionate kissing and touching, if not more? How can you go to local parties or spend a weekend with an older friend at the university without getting wasted? How can you travel in certain circles without sometimes getting high on drugs? It all feels good, it's socially acceptable, and you just know you aren't cool without sometimes giving in to the immoral impulses of your wild side.

These views actually belong to "naturalism," a theory that human nature is perfectly good in itself. Whatever impulses we feel, says naturalism, are good for us and may be followed without harm. If we feel the need for companionship, we should call up a friend. If we feel the need for solitude, we should take a walk in the woods. If we feel the need for food, we should go get some. If we feel the need for more alcohol, we should drink more and more. If we feel like having sex, we should go out and get it. (If we feel like killing someone, we should go ahead?) In general, if something feels good, do it. Whatever we find pleasurable is healthy. Denying ourselves pleasure is destructive because it is "repressing" our true nature. We should go about telling others not to be so uptight and worried about what adults and others think because they are repressed and want to repress you. Sex is perfectly natural, drugs and alcohol are liberating, all experience is good, so indulge.

But few of us are naturalists once we think about our drives with our minds instead of our hormones. Any one who has an ounce of brains, Herman Melville once wrote, recognizes the need of some notion like original sin to explain our actual situation and behavior. We can't rid ourselves of the sneaky suspicion that there is something twisted in the human condition. The warp seems obvious in the area, say, of personal relations. Although we can be very nice to people when we want to be, on other occasions we follow an impulse to be nasty. We cut down, we harass, we tell tales, we mock, we put people in their place. If we don't get an uneasy feeling about human nature when we do nasty things, we certainly get it when they are done to us. But if we are often off-base in these matters of justice and charity, if our will to dominate and show up others is so strong, won't indulgence of our other drives and passions be at least somewhat off? If we know we have to learn to control our temper because it gets us in trouble, why should we be surprised that we need to learn to control our sex drive?

Everyone's experience confirms the unnaturalness of misusing our natural drives. If we overindulge in food, we get stomach upset. If in alcohol, we get a hangover. The cost of self-indulgence in wrecked careers, wrecked families, and wrecked lives is more apparent every day. Alcoholism, drug abuse, teenage pregnancy, sexually transmitted disease, and an off-hand attitude toward divorce are seen increasingly as great social problems. It becomes ever harder to see drunks, druggies, and sex studs as more attractive and cooler than people who control themselves and have fun without dehumanizing themselves and others.

Still, everyone does it? Our drives' power to devour us requires that we resist such peer pressure if we are to survive as moral creatures. What can it be but physical, moral, and spiritual insanity when teens drink themselves into oblivion night after night, when certain fraternities fill and refill common vomit cans, when parties become sex orgies, when condoms and birth control pills are as common as aspirin? What glory do we really achieve by getting so continually drunk that we barely function as human beings at all? Is it really an enviable achievement to puke up our guts or to go catatonic on drugs? to engage in sexual activity with people we barely know, or with a long string of boyfriends or girlfriends? Are people who lose control of themselves really admirable? Hasn't something gone terribly wrong in men and women who shed their specifically human natures so thoughtlessly? some lack of an ideal or even reason for living?

The Church confirms our actual experience of the split in human nature. God gives us our natural drives, the Church tells us, and so all are good in themselves. In fact, each has a specific and important purpose. Without food and drink, we die. Without sex, the race dies. Without the drive for experience, we would never study or learn anything and would live pretty much as potatoes.

But original sin and our own sins have twisted these needs and drives so that they tend to overflow their proper channels. Our minds, hearts, and wills do not easily or constantly control them. Given full rein, they can completely enslave us so that the more we get, the more we want. They can destroy rather than construct our human personality. Apart from the issue of alcohol and drug addiction, we can wonder how anyone could sink so low as to wake up most Sunday mornings on the bathroom floor, or spend their Friday nights cruising for drugs and pickups. Yet we all tend to become slaves to our passions and drives. They can take us prisoner before we know the war has begun. They can possess us like demons or aliens.

Note that even lesser addictions, for example, the so-called "recreational" use of marijuana, do others and us harm. They weaken or, perhaps, ruin not just our physical health, but the power of our minds and wills. Overindulging ourselves, we risk losing the best part of ourselves. The more we seek ourselves self-centeredly in our animal needs, the less charitable, reliable, cheerful, human we become.

The Church condemns such excesses precisely because we become less morally and humanly responsible, more distant from the image of God and Christ in our mind and will, more deliberately escapist, not from the everyday grind, but from the Christian universe. Let's look at the specific case of alcohol, certainly a prime area of overindulgence for many teens.

Catholics are not forbidden alcoholic drinks. The Church sees alcohol as a product of God's creation that can help people to celebrate, relax, open up with each other, and take a break, for a time, from the consciousness of pressing business or problems. Alcohol, rightly used, has a positive personal and social effect, one which, we may say, Christ sanctified by providing the good wine at the marriage party in Cana. At the same time, we should respect the many people who don't care to drink or can't. We have to know ourselves also. There are those don't like alcohol, those who can take it or leave it, and those who love it. You must be very careful if you're in the last category. (According to the National Institute on Alcohol Abuse and Alcoholism, one in every thirteen adults abuses alcohol!)

Deliberate overindulgence in alcohol is a sin because it robs us of rational control, weakens our will, and often leads to other sins. Indeed, a recent report indicates that a very large percentage of crimes committed on college campuses—everything from theft to assault to rape—are alcohol related. Intoxication dehumanizes us. Consider how our healthy nature rebels against it. Psychologically, we may become depressed and dissatisfied with our lot, imprudently unrestrained in our judgments, emotions, and actions. We may insult our best friends, pick fights with innocent strangers, try to pick up obnoxious acquaintances. Physically, we become gradually uncoordinated, unintelligible, and unconscious. We have lost our manhood or womanhood, not proved it, made fools of ourselves, not heroes. Yet stupidly, like sheep that never learn that eating clover literally blows their stomachs up, we may keep drinking that day or the next, thinking that more of the same will satisfy us. Through a bad hangover, nature tries to show us the madness of it, but some of us don't learn the lesson very easily. (Nor do drug users seem to learn from the similar and worse effects of their habit.)

Of course, both cultural pressure and peer pressure intensifies our naturally strong tendency to self-indulge. Ads tell us that drinkers get beautiful partners and excel in competition. Our "friends" encourage us and may even praise us for getting totally smashed. "Man, you were sooooo wasted—it was awesome!" Awesome? These are our friends? people who care about us and so tell us the truth? If we give in, we make ourselves even more like sheep that follow the herd rather than think and act realistically.

Pride plays its part too. It helps us rationalize before and justify after we have overindulged, even when we know deep down that we are wrong. It urges us, in the name of our self-esteem, to stay down in the gutter when we have landed there. It prompts us to brag before our friends about our drinking (or drug use or sexual conquests, real or imagined), but to be ashamed to mention them to a priest or someone else who might remind us of their morality. Pride makes us pretend that the gutter is wonderful and glorious, and it keeps us there for fear of finding ourselves mistaken.

Being temperate in drink can be difficult at any age. But with God's grace, our honest effort, and common sense, teens can be good without being goody-goodies, keep true friends, and become badly-needed examples of attractive moderation who help the others. But, listen, if things are really bad, if you are a confirmed addict of any sort, I beg you, and Christ begs you, to drop those friends similarly addicted and to avoid those places where your addiction feeds. Seek the professional medical and spiritual help you need to recover from what you simply must finally recognize as a destructive disease.

Sexual Realism

Although we've referred to the virtues of purity and chastity several times already, we now need to talk about sexual morality in detail. Without question, this is the area that teenagers generally have the most difficulty in living. Not only are our hormones kicking in, but also we're suddenly surrounded by peers and media who seem obsessed with sex. All of these factors make keeping control a challenge.

On the other hand, as teens, we sometimes forget that self-control, especially in sexual matters, is almost as much of a challenge for adults as it is for us. A friend once told me how startled he was when he first realized this:

> Going to a major college in the late sixties made you think that you had seen and heard everything. Certainly, coming from a small town, I thought nothing back there could surprise me. But during a visit home, my father, not once, but twice managed to shock me.
>
> He was complaining about riding the subways into the city, and I thought that it must be the noise and crowds that bothered him more as he got older. No, he said, it was the girls in the ultra-short mini-skirts, which were then popular. Well, I suggested, the changing public morals were a problem for many older people in those days. No, he returned, that wasn't it. He just found it harder to keep his eyes off all those pretty little things. It had never occurred to me that my Dad could have the same lecherous impulses that could plague me.
>
> Later, out of the blue, Dad began reflecting on his marriage of nearly thirty years. Uh oh, I thought, he's going to turn senti-mental on me. No, just the observation that he had never cheated on my mother, and he was sure she had never cheated on him. My parents cheating on one another! The idea wasn't even possible! I had never even considered that my parents' fidelity required a continually renewed commitment to one another, that

they were free to break that bond but had freely chosen to preserve it, despite the years, difficulties, and hordes of mini-skirted young ladies and handsome young men. I never imagined that occasional tugs of the flesh, the passions, and temptations could be a normal part of my parents' lives as they were of mine.

My friend's story may help us keep things in perspective. As teens, we sometimes think older people don't understand our attractions and drives. True, they may have forgotten how strong these can be during the teen years, but, more often, they caution us because they remember only too well how it was and are still fighting for control themselves. We are not, as we sometimes think as teens, special beings who are experiencing and discovering things never known before. Rather, we are awakening to drives and feelings that are the common inheritance of adult humanity.

We pretend indulgence in sex is different, more normal than other indulgences. We can see the effects of overindulgence in alcohol and drugs very clearly. But, despite the epidemics of AIDS and HIV, as well as other sexually transmitted diseases and teen pregnancies, we fool ourselves into thinking we can get away scot-free with sexual indulgence. While the medical profession regularly denounces the evils of tobacco, alcohol, and drugs, it seldom discourages sexual indulgence but rather preaches how to indulge "safely."

But the Church continues to condemn any deliberate stimulation of sexual pleasure outside marriage. Why? Because of the real nature of people and of sex. For the Church, the sexual instinct is a God-given good, a drive that is essential for the preservation of the race, and for uniting a married couple in the mutual self-giving that is essential for family life. Because sex is so crucial to the race, and to sustaining the family, God has necessarily made it a strong, pleasurable drive in individuals.

So much about sex is strictly part of our animal nature and as crucial to the survival of rabbits as it is to us. But in the sexual instinct, the Church also sees a truly awesome sharing in God's creative power.

Our offspring are not rabbits, but human beings with souls and the potential to be free children of God and heirs to God's Kingdom. Genes cannot make the spirit within us, which reflects God because it can know and love and endure beyond the death of the body. Only God can give such a spirit. But God ties God's own hands so that God cannot create a new soul without the cooperation of a man and woman in the sexual act. And that very act is a sign of love and commitment that are so deep they are lifelong—and lived out in marriage. Far from being negative on sex, the Church holds it among the most sacred things of life and thus condemns its misuse through masturbation, artificial birth control, premarital sex, homosexual acts, and the like, as objectively serious sins against God's creation. If a teenage couple claims to be in love, is being careful not to have a child, and simply wants to enjoy each other, the Church answers that the couple is putting the cart before the horse. Basically and unarguably, we have the drive to have children and to create loving, lasting families.

In fact, the Church is here, as everywhere else, the realist. It insists on marriage before sex for several reasons. First, God clearly intended that a man and woman should become as "one flesh," implying a stability that only the institution of marriage provides. Second, the public act and covenant of marriage should help people generally to stay faithful to their lifelong commitment through all its ups and downs. Third, kids come no matter how "safe" a couple thinks they are. And kids need parents—both parents—to be there for them as they grow.

Just as important, sex also becomes the highest physical expression of love between a married man and woman who have become one, who have committed themselves totally to each other. The Christian married couple can enjoy the sexual act immensely and often. The Church also points out the obvious: how short-lived this pleasure of the body is compared with the continuous pleasure of mind and heart in true friendship and love. In fact, she requires not only that the sexual act remain open to the possibility of children but also that it be a reaffirmation of the couple's love for each other. In other words, it should not be a selfish act of lust.

"But you, beloved, must remember the predictions of the apostles of our Lord Jesus Christ; for they said to you, 'In the last time there will be scoffers, indulging their own ungodly lusts.' It is these worldly people, devoid of the Spirit, who are causing divisions" (Jude 1:17–19). Of course, as we would expect from Christ's warnings about the "world's hatred," contemporary naturalism resists these ideas on sex just as the old pagan world did. After all, it argues, our bodies are our own. Just as a woman has a "right" to reject a "foreign substance" like a baby from her body through abortion, so all of us have a "right" to experience sexual pleasure in any way we see fit. We may get our kicks through masturbation, heterosexual or homosexual pairing, adultery, oral sex, or whatever, so long as we and our partners do it freely and without hurting others.

This argument obviously appeals to our love of individual freedom. But it completely ignores, among other things, the Christian sense of the body as God-given and sanctified for specific purposes. Saint Paul, in fact, bluntly insists that "The body is meant not for fornication but for the Lord. . . . Do you not know that your bodies are members of Christ? Should I therefore take the members of Christ and make them members of a prostitute? Never!" (1 Corinthians 6:13–15). Further on in the same passage, he reminds us that "your body is a temple of the Holy Spirit," whose presence and teachings should guide us in using it. "You are not your own," he concludes, "for you were bought with a price"—that of Christ's blood. "Therefore, glorify God in your body" (1 Corinthians 6:19–20). Our bodies are not our own and have less meaning than a rabbit's if we cut them off from God's purposes. Thus, Paul includes misuses of sex, that some tried to justify in his time as now, among the sins that exclude people from the Kingdom of God: "Do you not know that wrongdoers will not inherit the kingdom of God? Do not be deceived! Fornicators, idolaters, adulterers, male prostitutes, sodomites, thieves, the greedy, drunkards, revilers, robbers—none of these will inherit the kingdom of God" (1 Corinthians 6:9–10). As the context makes clear, he means those who do not repent of such sins will lose heaven.

Another naturalistic argument appeals to our belief in progress and technology. Humans have dominated nature through science and invention so that it serves us and makes life more pleasurable and productive. We now have a technology that can not only prevent conception, but also actually mimic it in a test tube. Why not allow science to prevent unwanted pregnancies? Why not let it help those couples who can't have a child on their own? Medical technology has made so many other miracles realities. Just consider the various transplants, drugs, and artificial limbs that take over for nature. The Church seems to be persecuting Galileo once again in not recognizing such beneficial powers.

This argument is glaringly naive about the automatic blessings of all technological advance—Hiroshima alone should give us grave pause. But it also denies the divine source of life's sacredness. It ignores the distinction between technology that complements or supplements the body's God-given nature and purposes, and technology that undermines them. It is one thing for a drug to stimulate antibodies against a disease attacking the body's integrity and quite another to prevent the natural development of the embryo, to abort it, as the morning-after pill and some contraceptives do, or to fertilize many more eggs than we can possibly implant in the womb, knowing that we will later destroy the excess ones—each a living, separate individual.

Teens must also be aware of the influence of the "romantic" view of sex in books, movies, and, sometimes, in our dreams. Two people, unmarried or perhaps married to other people, have terrific chemistry and affection for each other, says this view, so it is good and beautiful that they make love. You can't call such acts sins of fornication or adultery because they are so "right." Wrong! For all the reasons we just went through, such acts, even seen through the unreal golden haze of the big screen or the romance novel, remain sins, no matter what our feelings about them. We need to be aware that tenderness can lead to a misuse of sex as easily as lust can—in fact, more easily in some of us.

Similarly, the Church teaches that homosexual acts, even in the context of a loving relationship, are morally wrong because they are closed to new life. God intended sexuality to enrich the married love between a man and a woman; any other use of our sexuality is a misuse of it. It's essential to understand that homosexual acts are sinful—not homosexuals themselves. Many persons with homosexual tendencies are careful not to misuse their sexuality, just like many other unmarried people. We must show respect and avoid unjust discrimination, against all people, including those with homosexual or other nontraditional sexual tendencies.

For a teen, of course, actually living by the Church's teaching on sexuality is more than just a matter of arguments and counter-arguments. We feel the pressure of the drive, newly awakened from within, as well as the anti-Christian social and peer pressure from without. The Church understands our weakness, environment, and occasional confusion because Christ understands it. But Christ and his Church also tell us to seek the truth first, to learn what is right and wrong. The Pope and bishops reaffirm it regularly. The Church tells us to turn to a trustworthy source for the true teaching.

Yes, ask your real questions about temptations, thoughts, and acts, without embarrassment, of a good priest or some other Catholic you can trust. Obviously, we need to know what is sinful to avoid it. But we also need to know what are simply facts of fallen human nature and not sinful in themselves. Otherwise, many well-intentioned teens can become scrupulous or depressed about things they are not guilty of. We should understand that the wildest thoughts and tempta-tions can enter our minds and the most uncomfortable feelings can afflict us unbidden. Those do not become sinful unless we consent to them, either feeding them or acting on them. It is not, for example, uncommon to have occasional feelings of attractions for members of the same sex during adolescence. Such feelings in themselves are not sinful and do not mean that we are homosexual—although I think an unfortunate number of young people are misled into thinking so because they don't talk about this experience. The point is to ask about things that bother or confuse you.

Such Christian sources can also tell us the means to overcome bad habits. Masturbation, for example, can become a regular and discouraging temptation for some teens. But experiencing this temptation also can become an occasion to draw closer to our Lord and to rely more on God's grace. To combat this and other sexual sins, we can seek forgiveness, strength, and hope in prayer, the sacrament of Penance, and the Eucharist. We can learn to practice small self-denials in eating, drinking, working, and socializing that toughen our wills and unite us more with Christ's cross and his victory over death. We can try to do all of God's will for us by filling our day with acts of prayer and service in our family and social life, work, and recreation—so that we haven't even the time or energy to think about ourselves and self-indulgence. We can get to know ourselves as God knows us, recognizing and reacting to those moments of tiredness and weakness, those moods of grief and gloom that leave us more prone to self-indulgence. We are, after all, called to Christian maturity, and that means a real and courageous struggle against temptations. In areas of chastity, particularly, we need to fight against a wayward curiosity. Of course, there is a natural curiosity about sex when we're adolescents and, hopefully, you asked your parents or other trustworthy adults about it when you were younger.

But even when we've got a basic biological knowledge, we can still tend to look for cheap thrills, which may not be serious sins in themselves but can easily lead to them. So a good battle plan will include avoiding those people, places, or things that promote sins against purity. Obviously, taking a break from the computer would be a good idea when we are tempted to visit that pornography Web site we've heard about. But, we also need to know ourselves and the particular things that are apt to turn us on, above and beyond what would turn anyone on. A certain TV show has nothing really objectionable about it that I can put my finger on but still somehow bothers me—so I should avoid it.

May I also mention again the most common occasion of falling into sins of impurity? Drinking. If drinking and driving don't mix, drinking and dating mix even less. The more we drink, the less we're in control of our thoughts and actions, and the more likely we are to give in to a sexual self-indulgence, which we'll later regret. Some estimate that drinking plays a role in two-thirds of teen pregnancies, and in three-quarters of date rapes. And, girls, even if it isn't rape— offering a few drinks is the oldest guy-on-the-prowl trick in the book.

Living Temperance

Exercising temperance, especially when we're young, can be like trying to control a great wild horse: you're in the saddle, you have the reins and a superior intellect, and yet the power of the horse is overwhelming. Having a full schedule, keeping busy, thinking of and serving others, avoiding or fleeing tempting situations, refusing arousing conversations and media offerings, learning to say no to whims, and similar practices are all necessary to live temperance.

But our own efforts are not enough. Alone, the Church tells us, it is impossible to live chastely and temperately in our environment. In fact, all "our help is in the name of the Lord" (Psalm 124:8). We need God's grace to fulfill duties and to obtain blessings that are beyond our feeble powers. We receive grace through the sacraments, especially the Eucharist and Penance, our own prayer and that of others, sacrifice, devotion to Mary, spiritual direction, and all the proven supernatural means. You can find a more detailed discussion on this topic in another book in this series, *Teens and Spirituality*. Grace reinforces our natural virtues. The Church teaches that when the Holy Spirit resides in our souls in grace, the Spirit brings a host of gifts, like a rich and kindly relative visiting a poor and large family. Among them are the infused moral virtues, which, if we don't place obstacles in the way, allow us always to judge and act in keeping with our faith. Other gifts of the Spirit also aid nature. Wisdom, counsel, and understanding, for example, perfect supernatural prudence, while a healthy fear of the Lord's just sentence spurs on fortitude.

"My little children, I am writing these things to you so that you may not sin. But if anyone does sin, we have an advocate with the Father, Jesus Christ the righteous" (1 John 2:1). Don't give in, Christ and the Church tell us, but . . . any of us can slip up and go overboard. If you do sin against purity or any other area of temperance, even in ways you think would surprise others, don't stay down for shame or embarrassment. Get up, regain your personhood, reassert your command over your drives and lives. Admitting the fault to ourselves, to God, and, if seriously sinful, to the priest in the sacrament of Penance enables us to begin again. The priest has heard it all, and much more, in these areas than most of us are able to imagine. Like Christ, he wants to forgive us and get us on our feet again. The only real shame and embarrassment is not to have the guts and humility to admit our sins and faults sincerely and to begin again.

One final point that can help a lot on a practical level but that we often forget is that we must learn to laugh at ourselves and especially at our self-indulgence. Sinning in these areas is no laughing matter. But it will help us to avoid sinning and to recover when we have sinned, if we can recognize our own foolishness in letting these passions control us. I do not mean that we should laugh at sex as a sharing in God's creative power. But we should laugh at the absurdities into which we allow sex and the other drives to lead us. Laughter at absurd images will help us to ridicule ourselves, if necessary, when we are so tempted. Nothing I have read so punctures the balloon of self-important self-indulgence as one of Bill Cosby's routines in which he imitates, hilariously, the different kinds of drunks and mocks the "intensifying power" of cocaine.

Scaling the Depths

The widespread self-indulgence of teens (and adults) in sex, drinking, and drugs often seems basically escapist. But what are we trying to escape from? Obviously, our fallen nature, the temptations of our culture, and the pace of modern living all put pressures on us. Some of us may have a greater genetic tendency to addiction. Moods, loneliness, failures can urge us to lose ourselves in physical pleasures. But common sense also tells us that many people seek excessive escape because they find little or no meaning in their ordinary lives. Sometimes we feel that we're so much "dust in the wind" that is blown this way and that for a short time by events we cannot control, and then we're released to settle and to mix indistinguishably with the other dirt. Teen self-indulgence often masks a lack of self-esteem and a self-destructive tendency that reveal themselves most disturbingly in anorexia, cutting, and the ultimate escape of suicide.

Certainly, if we are experiencing clinical depression, which is characterized by long-term feelings of hopelessness and listlessness, we need to seek professional help. Teen depression is a serious problem, and it often responds well to medication and talk therapy. You may be aware that flu, other illnesses, the dark months of winter, and poor diet and exercise can all cause varying degrees of depression, but many teens experience a kind of depression that's more like "the blues." Temperance as controlling or at least minimizing the effects of such feelings is critical. We can't always control the feelings themselves, but consciously dwelling on those feelings so that they overwhelm our mind and will is a lack of temperance. To feel hatred for the real evil someone has committed against others or us is normal. To wish and pray that person well, despite those feelings, is

Christian charity and temperance. In the same way, we can dislike negative aspects of our behavior or character but we don't need to beat ourselves up for them.

Adults sometimes mock the worries and crises of teens. "What are you so down about? Just wait until you really have some responsibilities to get frustrated about." Well, as teens we do tend to exaggerate normal ups and downs. Still, they are very real to us. A bad grade on an exam that we thought we aced, rejection by someone we ask out, the laughter at our honest attempt in some extracurricular activity, the misery of losing a boyfriend or girlfriend, the clamps that our parents might set on us too tightly—all such failures and frustrations affect us as much as larger tragedies do adults, because those kinds of failures may be the only tragedies we know.

Frustration, dejection, and occasional feelings of worthlessness are facts of human consciousness. Those who by temperament tend to be moody can be hellish companions. Christ and his Church recognize and accept those facts, as they do all others. They see such psychological and biological states as the result of original sin and of real limitations that we may exaggerate because of wounded pride. But, like all temptations, they are also the raw material for sanctification. To recognize the danger signals and avoid situations that could provoke excessive escape, to fight against the dark thoughts as best we can, to accept and live through them when we can't shake them, to maintain our Christian convictions and practices despite emotional blows, to open our hearts to a trusted adviser—all of these responses require grace, virtues, and an effort that Jesus will not fail to reward. Here especially we need the Holy Spirit's gifts of faith, hope, and charity.

Faith. Without faith in Christ's teaching about the value of doing God's will in every moment, this life would seem pretty worthless. Without faith in the Resurrection, in our own call to intimate, everlasting life with the Trinity, despair might seem reasonable. But if we really have faith, we should be able to put all our frustrations and difficulties into perspective. They are really of small importance in a world that passes as quickly as this one. God shows Martha this true perspective on life: "Martha, Martha, you are worried and distracted by many things; there is need of only one thing" (Luke 10:41–42). That one thing is union with our Lord. The only real tragedy is sin, which parts us from friendship with Christ and a share in his life. And sin only remains a tragedy if we despair and refuse to seek God's forgiveness.

Still, resisting the negative pull of our emotions is not easy. Perhaps only a great effort of the will and of prayer over time will enable us to accept hard events—the death of a family member or friend, for example—simply and humbly as reminders that we are just creatures and depend on God. This can be part of the cross for us. Saint Paul, who endured imprisonments, scourgings, stonings, shipwrecks, and so many other sufferings (see 2 Corinthians 11:23–28), finally thought he could take no more. But our Lord answered Paul's despairing prayer: "My grace is sufficient for you, for power is made perfect in weakness" (2 Corinthians 12:9). God never commands the really impossible, the Church teaches, or tempts us beyond what we can really handle, if we rely on God and make an effort.

Hope. "Humble yourselves therefore under the mighty hand of God. . . . Cast all your anxiety on him, because he cares for you." (1 Peter 5:6–7). We need the theological virtue of hope to contend with the downers of life and with the desire to escape and to resent them. Hope opposes both despair and pride. Both extremes ignore the help God has promised, that God must provide or fail to be God. Both assume, self-centeredly, that we can do it all on our own. Pride says, "I don't need God's help or anyone else's to do the right thing" or "God is good and won't condemn me no matter what I do." Despair says, "I've tried and tried but can't do it. There's no way I can do it." Pride escapes the demands of the Gospel by pretending they aren't there or don't apply to us. Despair escapes them by deciding they are impossible.

I believe that for every easygoing Christian teen who simply ignores Christ, there is another who takes him seriously but despairs of pleasing him. "I can't be good, so I might as well be bad," such young people think. They fail to take into account God's great mercy and God's grace. They have become so self-absorbed that goodness seems impossible. Often such teens are frustrated, naive idealists, who expect too much of themselves and, unlike Saint Paul, are too proud to accept their weaknesses and limitations—or, even worse, to accept Christ's acceptance of their weaknesses and limitations. They forget Saint Paul's words: "I will boast all the more gladly of my weaknesses, so that the power of Christ may dwell in me" (2 Corinthians 12:9).

The answer to failure, frustration, and misery, then, must also be rooted in our love for God but, even more importantly, in our recognizing God's love for us. "For God so loved the world that he gave his only Son, so that everyone who believes in him may not perish but may have eternal life" (John 3:16). Jesus loves us! He loves us, knowing full well how often we have failed and will fail him as friends. If he can accept our failures, why can't we? Let us shake off our proud self-pity. Let us love ourselves with all our faults as God loves us, not because we are perfect human beings or Christians, but because, however tarnished, we remain sons and daughters of God.

Rejoice Always!

If we pray and work to fight despair's various forms with faith, hope, and charity, we will have interior peace and joy. "Do not let your hearts be troubled" Christ tells his Apostles, as he faces the horrors of his sufferings and death (John 14:1). "Enter into the joy of your master" are the words that reward the good and faithful servant (Matthew 25:21). "Peace be with you" is his customary greeting after the Resurrection (Luke 24:36). "Rejoice in the Lord always; again I will say, Rejoice," exults Saint Paul repeatedly (Philippians 4:4). We are, the Church tells us, an Easter people. Daily, in the Holy Mass, the whole

Church prays that our Lord "keep us free from sin and protect us from all anxiety as we wait in joyful hope" for his coming ("Communion Rite," *Sacramentary,* p. 563).

Such joy is not simply an abstract idea or vague feeling. True Christians can enjoy everything in life, no matter what sacrifices their family, work, or social relations may require. Our joy comes from knowing that all our labors and sufferings are most pleasing to a loved one. Grief, tears, and bitterness may afflict us. But with God's help and our own efforts, nothing will shake the deep conviction in our minds and hearts that "all things work together for good for those who love God" (Romans 8:28). If need be, we will weather the storm of our upsets and try, for the sake of others and of our own faith, to smile, to forgive and forget, to persevere, and to offer the emotional hurt up to God as penance. With God's help, we will not seek a false salvation in excessive self-indulgence.

But is it possible in real life to counter those strong blasts of emotions like anger and frustration, those eerie, despairing moments when we feel no one understands or cares? In fact, at first, it may be impossible to regain a healthy perspective, no matter how hard we try. But regain it we eventually will, even in the hardest matters, if we pray regularly. "Are any among you suffering?" asks Saint James. "They should pray" (James 5:13). We can extend the advice. If we are down, frustrated, troubled, or feeling lonely, rejected, misunderstood, let us pray. If we turn to Christ, telling him, in whatever words we want, what is bothering us, then gradually he will restore us to a humanly sane and supernaturally beneficial perspective.

We will play the role of that poor man in the Gospel whose son is possessed by a "spirit" that "dashes him down; and he foams and grinds his teeth and becomes rigid." What agony has this man felt, as he and his wife have helplessly watched their son, unable to speak, and subject to fits "from childhood"! How bitter and hopeless we might expect them to be! Indeed, the father now seems near the end of his rope because even the Apostles have been unable to cure his son. But our Lord tells him that "All things can be done for the one who believes," and "immediately the father of the child cried out, 'I believe; help my unbelief'" (Mark 9:14–26). I do have faith and hope, but not enough to endure this misery any longer. It's tearing my heart apart. Christ rewards his humble prayer by curing the possessed boy. He will do the same for us, no matter how much our moods or our experience of a fallen world's harshness possess us.

Helping Others

If my reflections on the ups-and-downs of teen experience hit home for you, then you should realize that they hit home for those around you. If you have any experience of the kinds of sensitivities, frustrations, discouragements, and "tragedies" that teens especially may have, then you should be more compassionate towards others. I don't mean we should be like those teens (and adults) who have advice for everyone about everything but can't seem to straighten their own lives out. But, as we discuss at length in another book in this series, *Teens and Relationships*, we should be concerned about the downs of our friends and acquaintances. Here we just want to focus on helping those who are particularly troubled in a certain moment or even regularly.

Sometimes, of course, people simply need to be kidded out of their self-pity. They are taking themselves too seriously or blowing things way out of proportion. At other times, they just need someone to hear them out. They don't really want or need long speeches of advice but words of simple understanding, sympathy, and encouragement. If people they trust and like aren't there when they've got something on their minds, they may indeed feel isolated and alone in a cruel world.

Often we can suggest possible remedies, including spiritual ones, from our own experience to struggling friends. Even if these suggestions seem obvious clichés that our friends have heard adults say a thousand times before, they will have much more of an impact coming sincerely from another teen. It is one thing for your mother to insist you'll get over a lost love and quite another for a friend to do so. We must be especially careful with troubled souls not to get out of our depth. Are we telling them what is good for them or only what they want to hear? Do we ourselves have any real perspective on problems in this area, or should we advise our friend to seek help from a parent, teacher, guidance counselor, priest, or some other adult? Should we, without betraying our friend's confidence, ask a third party's advice about the whole business? In some cases, the real root of despair or disorientation is moral, and the best thing we can do for a friend is get them to a good priest to talk or go to confession—or, if our friend is not Catholic, to whatever his or her religion provides as an aid.

Does this person need professional help? We know that many of the mental or emotional disorders that used to be considered wholly psychological actually indicate a chemical imbalance in the brain. (Whether the imbalance is cause or effect of the problem is not yet clear.) In many cases, medication and changes in diet or lifestyle can cure depression or at least make it less crippling. (It goes without saying that medication must be prescribed by a physician who will carefully monitor the effects—don't even think about passing pills around!) But ultimately, all suffering is a personal, spiritual issue, for Christ alone can put our real and imaginary pains into true perspective. Very often our Lord seems to permit emotional crises to jolt us out of our complacency and to lead us to a greater knowledge of and commitment to God. God does the same to those around us and may want us to help them see God's purpose. Do we really believe that the life of the soul is primary? Do we really desire to enjoy our friends' companionship forever in heaven? Do we really want them to be happy and to avoid the permanent despair and misery that is hell? Then we must talk about spiritual perspectives with them now and steer them to others who can help preserve that supernatural life and make it bloom.

MORAL
HEROES

So, there you have it. Some kind of overview of the moral life, on paper.

But, of course, morality is useless on paper. We need to decide to translate it into action. Let me stress it again. We must really want to become good, moral, virtuous people. Our moral health is ultimately in our own hands. Daily, we experience that our freedom plays a terrifyingly real role in our destiny. An Old Testament passage says so simply and starkly:

> It was he who created humankind in the beginning,
>> and he left them in the power of their own free choice.
> If you choose, you can keep the commandments,
>> and to act faithfully is a matter of your own choice.
>
> . . . .
>
> Before each person are life and death,
>> and whichever one chooses will be given.

If we make a habit of choosing good, if we are regularly obedient to the moral law for love of God and neighbor, if we try to live a virtuous life, then we will continually increase the life of God's grace in us until we are ready to breathe the absolutely free, fresh air of heaven. If we make a habit of choosing evil, if we regularly and unrealistically put our own petty egos before the realities of God and neighbor, then we will lose the life of God in us. Yes, we have to make a deep-down decision to live morally—which, remember, includes beginning again when we do fail. Otherwise, pressures from outside will overcome us and make us slaves to all kinds of sins. Otherwise, we become chameleons, lizards who change our moral attitudes and behavior depending on who's with us. Chameleons will not change the world into a civilization of love. They will be changed themselves into the world's civilization of greed, conflict, materialism, and death.

We should expect our Christian morality to clash with the unchristian world's behavior. Our Lord told us it would, and Saint Paul bears witness to this reality from the start.

> Now this I affirm and insist on in the Lord: you must no longer live as the Gentiles live, in the futility of their minds. They are darkened in their understanding, alienated from the life of God because of their ignorance and hardness of heart. They have lost all sensitivity and have abandoned themselves to licentiousness, greedy to practice every kind of impurity. (Ephesians 4:17–19)

Rather, must we "lead lives worthy of the Lord, fully pleasing to him," as we "bear fruit in every good work and . . . grow in the knowledge of God" (Colossians 1:10). If we do so "in the midst of a crooked and perverse generation," we will "shine like stars in the world" (Philippians 2:15). We can survive and even transform such a society if we rely on God's grace and do what we can—which includes developing the virtues.

Really, as Christians, we must want to change the world, to make it more moral, more human, more Christian. So many around us are spineless chameleons, so many seem drugged by their enslavement to their passions, so many live for the moment like dumb animals. Through our friendship, our example, and conversation, we can help them live again as real humans, as real creatures of God.

To do so, our moral life can't be an occasional thing. It can't depend on our mood, our companions, or our circumstances. It can't be self-seeking, proud, or boorish. It will have to be central to our lives, more precious than life. It will have to be constant . . . daring . . . persevering . . . heroic.

Young people are attracted to adventure. Living a moral life, spreading the example of a moral life, is a great adventure—precisely because of the obstacles. It's harder to live the moral life day in and day out than it is to win the World Cup . . . to trek across the Sahara . . . to climb Mount Everest . . . to cross the Atlantic alone on a raft . . . to circle the globe in a hot air balloon.

Are you up for it? Do you have the guts? I mean, really? Our age does recognize moral heroes. Even many critics admire the personal qualities of John Paul II and the courage he shows in sticking to his convictions. Most of the secular moral heroes of the past century have been people like Solzhenitsyn in Russia, people who stood up to real political abuses at the risk of their own lives. But what we now need even more are everyday heroes of moral life, Christians of all ages who quietly go about doing the right thing consistently, no matter what the pressures from within or without. They are the opposite of wishy-washy chameleons. They are the great whales of the moral life who, whether the waters around them are Arctic or tropical, maintain a constant temperature of commitment behind their protective covering of grace and virtue. Their example and word can change the thinking and acting of those around them and, if enough of us are trying, a whole culture.

Impossible? How many of the early Christians can you name? A handful, at most. And yet all those anonymous, ordinary people contributed to transforming an empire that was possibly more pagan than our own world.

Come on, get radical, down to the roots. Be a real rebel, not the usual bogus stereotypical teen of books and films. Start the revolution . . . with yourself. Be part of this great crusade the popes have called to reseed the moral terrain around us with true love. Christ can show us how. As John Paul II said in his message at the 2001 World Youth Day in Rome, "With the truth of his words that sound hard but fill the heart with peace, Jesus reveals the secret of how to live a true life."

ACKNOWLEDGMENTS

The scriptural quotations contained herein are from the New Revised Standard Version of the Bible, Catholic Edition. Copyright © 1993 and 1989 by the Division of Christian Education of the National Council of the Churches of Christ in the United States of America. All rights reserved.

The excerpts and quotations labeled *Catechism of the Catholic Church* or *CCC* are adapted and quoted from the English translation of the *Catechism of the Catholic Church* for use in the United States of America, pages 496–497, numbers 1765, 1750, 1753, 1755, 1756, and 1859. Copyright © 1994 by the United States Catholic Conference, Inc.—Libreria Editrice Vaticana. Used with permission.

The quotation on page 86 is from the "Communion Rite," in the *Sacramentary,* English translation prepared by the International Commission on English in the Liturgy (New York: Catholic Book Publishing Co., 1985), page 563. English translation of *The Roman Missal* Copyright © 1973 by the ICEL, Inc. All rights reserved. Used with permission.

The quotation on page 91 is from "Message of the Holy Father to the Youth of the World on the Occasion of the XVI World Youth Day," *www.vatican.va/holy_father/john_paul_ii/messages/youth/documents/hf_jp-ii_mes_20010215_xvi-world-youth-day_en.html,* accessed September 8, 2004.

To view copyright terms and conditions for Internet materials cited here, log on to the home pages for the referenced Web sites.

During this book's preparation, all citations, facts, figures, names, addresses, telephone numbers, Internet URLs, and other pieces of information cited within were verified for accuracy. The authors and Saint Mary's Press staff have made every attempt to reference current and valid sources, but we cannot guarantee the content of any source, and we are not responsible for any changes that may have occurred since our verification. If you find an error in, or have a question or concern about, any of the information or sources listed within, please contact Saint Mary's Press.

Endnote Cited in Quotation from *Catechism of the Catholic Church*
1. Cf. *Mk* 3:5–6; *Lk* 16:19–31.